D1518058

PEACEPRINTS

Sister Karen's
Paths to Nonviolence

Evelyn McLean Brady, Editor

Commissioned by
Interfaith Peace Network of Western New York

BUFFALO
HERITAGE
UNLIMITED

Copyright © 2008 Interfaith Peace Network of Western New York

"I Leave PEACEPRINTS" words and logo are a registered trademark of the Sisters of St. Joseph, Buffalo, NY, and are used by Buffalo Heritage Unlimited, Inc. under permission of the Sisters of St. Joseph.

Printed and bound by the Zenger Group, Buffalo, New York in the United States of America.
ISBN 978–0–9788476–5–4

Cover design by George Schaeffer

Proceeds from this book will support the **Interfaith Peace Network of Western New York** to "assist faith communities in building a culture of peace" (info@ipnwny.org, 716–332–3904, www.ipnwny.org) and the **SSJ Sister Karen Klimczak Center for Nonviolence** whose mission is to "eliminate violence in ourselves, in our society, and in our world." (info@sisterkarencenter.org, 716–362–9688, www.sisterkarencenter.org).

"It would be hard to imagine a more fitting tribute to a beautiful life (and yes, death!) than PEACEPRINTS. *The authors of poetry, interviews, stories, the takers of photos, the artists left peaceprints for me. In dark days, these imprints illumine our way all the more vividly. Let us be grateful, ponder, and walk."*
- **Daniel Berrigan, SJ**

"The concept of nonviolence can be complex, misunderstood, and even dismissed. Reading PEACEPRINTS, *the reader will learn keys to living a life of nonviolence and compassion. We need this book."*
- **Sister Helen Prejean, CSJ**, author, *Dead Man Walking; The Death of Innocents: An Eyewitness Account of Wrongful Death*

"Sister Karen spent most of her life reaching out to those whom many of us wish would disappear–the penniless, the homeless, the ill, the addicted, the mad–until finally she became one more of the victims. Yet the way she lived—a Christ–haunted, Christ–centered life—has left no one who was privileged to have contact with her unchanged, as this small book bears witness."
- **Jim Forest**, chair, Orthodox Peace Fellowship; Former General Secretary, International Fellowship of Reconciliation

"How I rejoice in the life of God's precious instrument of peace, Sr. Karen, a lamb of God who lived Christ's teachings...until death. 'My peace I give you—peace I leave you.' PEACEPRINTS *should be imprinted on our hearts and lives."*
- **Mother Antonia** (Mexico's Prison Angel), ESEH, Servants of the 11th Hour, SJE

"These pages depict how Karen lived out her own personal prayer. As she writes in her journal, January 2003: 'Inspire me to take the right steps and give me the courage to follow through on what I know needs to be done.' *Reading this book will inspire and motivate you to respond unconditionally to the dimensions of mystery and courage in your life, to leave your own peaceprints."*
- **Sister Loretta Young**, President, Sisters of St. Joseph, Buffalo, New York

"The various writings herein give eloquent testimony that we, as individuals and in community, can emulate and perpetuate Sister Karen's peaceprints message every day by fulfilling the Great Commandment–loving God and loving our neighbor as our self–through any act of caring or selflessness. Sister Karen and these writings show us how."
- **Hon. John J. LaFalce**, Member of Congress (1975–2003)

"Sister Karen's inspiring life continues to resonate in Western New York and beyond. PEACEPRINTS *is a fitting tribute to her, as well as a way to keep her memory and her powerful message alive."*
- **Margaret Sullivan**, Editor, *The Buffalo News*

"Knowing Sister Karen is to know the nonviolent gospel in action. I recommend PEACEPRINTS *to all those who want to understand, as Sister Karen did, that active nonviolence–engaging others with respect, compassion, and love–is the only way to peace."*
- **Janet Chisholm**, Peace Coordinator and National Coordinator for Creating a Culture of Peace Nonviolence Training, Kirkridge Retreat and Study Center

"On behalf of the City of Buffalo, I am proud to endorse PEACEPRINTS *a book about Sister Karen, our city's great peacemaker. I commend the Interfaith Peace Network of Western New York for continuing its important mission of spreading the ideals of nonviolence."*
- **Byron Brown, Mayor of Buffalo New York**

Dedication

In thanksgiving for
Karen Klimczak, SSJ
whose life has hastened a nonviolent future

... and for all those who leave Peaceprints.

Contents

Part I–Biographies

Part II–Leaving Peaceprints

Witnesses to Peaceprints
Prison Ministry

Communities of Peaceprints
Organizations with Common Vision

Reflections of Peaceprints
Individual Responses to Sister Karen

Gifts of Peaceprints
Nonviolence and Mysticism

Acknowledgements

This book is the result of the dedication of the Interfaith Peace Network of Western New York to keeping alive the spirit and mission of Sister Karen Klimczak, SSJ. For their untiring commitment to this end, we are all indebted.

I am deeply grateful for the trust given to me to bring *PEACEPRINTS* to fruition. This was not a singular journey. Several members of the IPN served on the editorial board, which played a significant role in guiding the direction and purpose of the book, and which over the months became a supportive and caring community. Sister Karen would have approved.

Special thanks go to these editorial board members: to Jim Mang for his measured and wise guidance to assure that each aspect of this book authentically reflects Sister Karen and the community she served; to June Licence for her irrepressible affirmation of board members and their work, for her role as treasurer, and for her always gentle advice; to Joan English for her friendship, for her business acumen, for taking care of seemingly endless details, and for her help in selecting and preparing Sister Karen's journals for publication; to Sister Jean Klimczak, OSF, for providing essential documents, photos, and writings of Sister Karen, for her work on grants, for lightening our work in every way possible, for her listening heart and care for all of us; to Audrey Mang, for her participation as assistant editor, copy editor, and every other role she played to support this project. With her generous and kind spirit, no job was too large or too small, and her attention to detail was a gift.

Thank you to each writer who responded to one simple direction: write from your heart. They did not fail.

The word poet comes from the Greek meaning "to create." That is why I call George Schaeffer the poet of *PEACEPRINTS*. As the technical editor and graphic designer, George volunteered to create a book that would be worthy of Sister Karen. He has succeeded. No words can fully express my gratitude for his talent, his perseverance, his careful work. For the incomprehensible amount of time he generously gave throughout the nine months of this project–and for his sense of humor–I give heartfelt thanks.

When Marti Gorman, executive director of Buffalo Heritage Unlimited, became involved with *PEACEPRINTS*, she called it a "magnet for miracles," and she was one of the miracles. Marti volunteered to publish this book "to thank the Sisters of St. Joseph who played a very important role in my high school years." Marti's guidance has been invaluable, and we sincerely thank her. We also thank Dr. Joseph Bieron, CEO of Buffalo Heritage.

During the 2007 Christmas holiday, while visiting Buffalo from Seattle, Washington, Colleen Dunham inquired about the dove signs displayed throughout the city. She was told about Sister Karen's ministry and this book, and another miracle occurred. A professional indexer, Colleen immediately offered to index *PEACEPRINTS* as a gift. We send a bouquet of thanks to her and her company, Colleen Dunham Indexing, for the peaceprints she has left on this project.

I am indebted to Ramona Whitaker for demonstrating on the final manuscript that editing is a science and an art and to Jim Charlier for the "finishing touches" he gave to the book. Lisa Murray–Roselli, Kathy Zalocha, and Pat Nightengale helped me through some challenging writing terrain, and I am ever grateful. Chris Anspach was a treasure with her efficient transcription skills and sunny disposition.

Our deep gratitude goes also to the Sisters of St. Joseph and Associates, who graciously supported the creation of *PEACEPRINTS* and gave permission for the use of Sister Karen's journals and the term "peaceprints"; to Claire Rung, executive producer of Daybreak Productions, Catholic Diocese of Buffalo, for offering the Emmy–nominated *Apostle of Peace* DVD found in this book; and to the Sisters of Social Service, for their prayers and friendship while I went on retreat with *PEACEPRINTS*.

Sincerest thanks go to the Riefler Fund, the Rev. A. Joseph Bissonette Foundation, and Tom Waring for their generous financial support. We are deeply grateful as well to the Zenger Group for printing this book.

With great affection I thank my husband, Hugh Brady, who each and every day supported me as I carried out this sacred trust.

Evelyn McLean Brady
Editor

Introduction

The need to keep cherished memories is in the DNA of the human heart. The ways people hold their memories can be as unique as the memories themselves. Native Americans weave memories into basket designs. In some African tribes body scarification is an outward representation, a memory board, of family and tribal history. Slaves' spirituals encoded stories of their experience for future generations. From pioneer days to current times, quilters have sewn patches into blankets of treasured memories. Journals document incidents and feelings otherwise forgotten, and memoirs, biographies, and autobiographies safeguard the stories of who we are and why our lives have meaning. The ways memories are kept enhance the memories themselves.

The Interfaith Peace Network of Western New York chose to commission this book to remember Sister Karen Klimczak, SSJ, Buffalo's beloved champion of nonviolence, who dedicated her life to providing sanctuary and hope for ex–offenders and was killed on Good Friday in 2006 by one of the men she served. Sister Karen would not want this "memory keeper" to focus on her. She lived as one with the community she served, and that would be the context in which she would want to be remembered.

We asked individuals from various walks of life in Buffalo a simple question: "How did Sister Karen's life converge with your own?" This work, *PEACEPRINTS: Sister Karen's Paths to Nonviolence,* is their communal response. The biographies, stories, essays, interviews, poetry, art, and photographs contained within have been contributed by ex–offenders, clergy, women religious, and others affected by her prison ministry; by members of organizations who shared her vision; by those who loved her as a family member, as a Sister of St. Joseph, and as a friend; and by many others who have been moved by her selfless spirit. Interspersed with entries from Sister Karen's journals (which, whenever used, will appear in italics and include her creative punctuation), these writings invite us to learn from our sister Karen and from each other.

The book is divided into two parts. Part I provides an overview of Sister Karen's life and prison ministry. It introduces the major themes of mysticism, nonviolence, forgiveness, redemption, charity, and respect that governed her life. In Part II the community writings explore these themes. At the end of this book, reflection and discussion questions will provide opportunities for readers, individually or in groups, to explore the themes. Although the reader will find that different stories or essays may address the same events, the wider perspectives they provide both deepen and broaden our understanding of Sister Karen.

In preparing this book, it became clear that each writing–intentionally or not–resonated with the message of the Beatitudes that Jesus taught his disciples in the Sermon on the Mount:

3 Blessed are the poor in spirit, for theirs is the kingdom of heaven. 4 Blessed are those who mourn, for they shall be comforted. 5 Blessed are the meek: for they shall inherit the earth. 6 Blessed are they who hunger and thirst after righteousness, for they shall be satisfied. 7 Blessed are the merciful, for they shall obtain mercy. 8 Blessed are the pure in heart, for they shall see God. 9 Blessed are the peacemakers, for they shall be called the children of God. 10 Blessed are they who are persecuted for righteousness' sake, for theirs is the kingdom of heaven. 11 Blessed are you when men shall revile you and persecute you and utter all kinds of evil against you falsely on my account. 12 Rejoice, and be glad: for great is your reward in heaven, for so men persecuted the prophets who were before you. (Matt. 5:3–12, RSV).

In one of her journal entries, Sister Karen changed the word *Beatitude* into the phrase "'Be'attitude of Christ." Her unique separation of the word and the clear meaning conveyed by the phrase that our attitudes should be Christlike inspired Sister Karen to express this message through "peaceprints," her word for paths to nonviolence, the "walk" of the Beatitudes, and the way to bring about the Kingdom of God on earth.

In her last Christmas newsletter in 2005, Sister Karen first shared with supporters her understanding of "Christprints." Soon thereafter, she would call "Christprints" by the new name, peaceprints, and describe in writing examples of ways to leave "Christprints/peaceprints": *"Keep a promise, try to understand, examine your demands on others, give a soft answer, take arms against malice, think first about someone else, apologize if you are wrong, dismiss suspicion, replace it with trust, encourage youth, listen, be kind, welcome a stranger, be gentle, gladden the heart of a child, take pleasure in the beauty and wonder of this earth."*

Some may dismiss the concept of peaceprints as too simplistic but, for those who strive to leave peaceprints by eliminating physical, emotional, and psychological violence from their own lives and the lives of others, the challenge is complex and demanding. Sister Karen's legacy keeps us aware of this challenge of nonviolence and peaceprints with the signs she devised that are found throughout the city of Buffalo and surrounding areas: "NONVIOLENCE begins with ME!" and "I Leave PEACEPRINTS."

When mourners attending her funeral were given one of Sister Karen's dove–shaped "I Leave PEACEPRINTS" signs, they were in effect handed paths to nonviolence. The writings in this "memory keeper" are peaceprints, as well. We offer them to you.

Evelyn McLean Brady
Editor

Part I

Chronology

1943   Birth of Theresa Klimczak, October 27, 1943

1963   Profession of vows with Franciscan Sisters
of St. Joseph, Hamburg, NY

1970   BS degree in education, Westfield State University,
Westfield, MA

1979   MA degree in pastoral ministry, Loyola University,
Chicago, IL/clown ministry

1965–91   Teacher in Michigan, Massachusetts,
and Buffalo, NY

1979   Transfer to the Sisters of St. Joseph, Buffalo, NY

1985   HOPE House ministry for ex–offenders,
Transfiguration convent, Buffalo, NY

1989   HOPE House moved to St. Bartholomew rectory,
Buffalo, NY

1991   HOPE Hospitality House (1991–2006)

1996   Hope Van Service

1999   SS. Columba–Brigid Teen Center, Buffalo, NY

2003   Re-dedication of HOPE House as Bissonette House

Pledge to Nonviolence service

2004   Pledge to Nonviolence service renamed
Remembering and Pledging

2005   "NONVIOLENCE begins with ME!"
lawn signs distributed

Prayer vigils for homicide victims

Days of Peace Dove in front of Bissonette House

2006   April 14, Good Friday: Sister Karen murdered

April 22, Sister Karen's funeral
("I Leave PEACEPRINTS" signs distributed)

SISTER KAREN KLIMCZAK, SSJ
MYSTIC, CLOWN, and SERVANT OF GOD

By Joan Albarella and Karen Whitney

As a contemporary mystic, Sister Karen Klimczak, SSJ, revealed God's love to others, especially the broken and hurting. She was God's goodness and light to those who needed compassion and forgiveness. We find in Sister Karen Klimczak's journals a deep sense of purpose and commitment to God. Her faith, courage, and resourcefulness allowed her to accomplish what most fear to attempt. The following journal entry reveals the joy and gratitude Sister Karen experienced: *I am so grateful for all that life has touched me with/the smiles and tears/the gentle rains and ferocious storms/the sunshine and the dark clouds./I always loved the challenges of life because they brought me so much closer to the Lord, who always held me in His arms.*

Such spiritual perception is not unique to Sister Karen, but it became the driving force of her ministry. The Dalai Lama has said, "Take into account that great love and great achievement involve great risk." There is no doubt that Sister Karen learned this lesson well.

Sister Karen was not born knowing that she would become a modern–day mystic, a clown of God, or a living force for nonviolence through the peaceprints she created and helped to nourish. She was born with inquisitiveness and inventiveness that often became a mixed blessing. Her large family was the first community to encourage and support her future calling to serve others.

Theresa Klimczak, Sister Karen's given name, was born on October 27, 1943, in Lackawanna, New York. She attended her parish elementary school and excelled in all her studies. Theresa felt a special kind of joy when she saw clowns, and she enjoyed the laughter of Clarabelle the Clown on the *Howdy Doody* television show. It was a foreshadowing of the future, like seeds planted for a future spring.

In 1978 Sister Karen began to water and cultivate those seeds. She was attending graduate school at Loyola University in Chicago when she joined ANAWIM, the campus liturgical performing arts company. Perhaps she was attracted by the name. *"Anawim"* (from Hebrew) are the poor, afflicted, humble, and meek for whom Jesus had such compassion. Certainly Sister Karen was also learning through prayer to become one of those she would eventually go on to serve.

As a member of the university performing arts group, she learned the art of clowning and, in studying the theology of clowning, was immediately drawn to its principles: "to make a personal decision to let oneself be transformed, to be childlike, to give of oneself, to elevate others to a position of worth, and to communicate clearly that everyone is loved."

In a simplified form, clown theology contains several elements of mysticism. The

1

American mystic Thomas Merton was drawn to the Zen experience because of the Zen clown. He discovered that the Zen clown possessed the self–transcending freedom experienced by contemplatives throughout the history of the Church.

Sister Karen began her journey of transformation by creating Bounce, her Clown of God. Bounce became the outward reflection of her inner mysticism. Her full clown regalia epitomized dying to oneself and being transformed by the Mystery of Christ. When she became Bounce, she could become the love of God for others.

Mystics believe that their relationship with God needs communication and response in order to grow. They believe that God desires their deepest self to be transformed. God's unconditional love is light. Light is knowledge and knowledge is faith. Sister Karen's life was a reflection of her desire for an unrestricted, unconditional love and total commitment to God.

Sister Karen's clown ministry is detailed in the article "Colorful Clowning at Camp Promise" by Thea Jarvis (1981). It explains how Bounce the Clown began each visit in partial whiteface. As she turned herself into Bounce, Sister Karen would begin with a prayer: "Oh, God, is that what you want me to do, God? You want me to cover myself all up so the special person inside me can come out?"

Sister Karen would then cover all her features with whiteface and use her "lipstick lovestick" to paint a big smile around her lips that helped her "speak kindly to people." A magic eyebrow pencil helped her eyes to "see deep down inside others."

"I'm afraid I'm going to get lost, God," she would say, as she put on her large, red nose. "Oh, God, I'll do that. Now I can follow you, God, wherever you lead me."

The colors of her red and yellow pig–tailed wig were symbolic: red for love and yellow for joy. She would say, "A new person is coming through," as she placed her "kindness hat" on her head, now ready to "walk in kindness" for the Lord.

Her new name "Bounce" was always spelled out with the bouncing of a ball, each letter a lesson, each letter a peaceprint, each letter a step in Sister Karen's journey:

B	"Be Yourself, Be Truthful."
O	"Others and How We Should Act Toward Others."
U	"Use the Gifts God Has Given You."
N	"Never Hurt Anyone."
C	"Be a Caring Person."
E	"Everyone Is Special."

Bounce, Sister Karen's clown of God, tried to "bounce love, joy, and peace to everyone." Bounce symbolized her transformation into a mystic of God and was an acronym for her life.

BOUNCE
Be Yourself, Be Truthful

B stands for "Be Yourself, Be Truthful." Sister Karen spent much of her life praying for affirmation of her truthfulness or the truth of her being. She rejoiced knowing that God accepted her just as she was. It takes a strong continuous prayer life, courage, and honesty to accept oneself. Truthfulness involves acknowledging who we really are and who we have become.

St. Teresa of Avila was sixty–two years old when she wrote her spiritually inspired book, *The Interior Castle*. The first dwelling place spoken of in the book refers to the spirituality of our early years. Sister Karen, whose given name Theresa was the same as the Saint of Avila's (although spelled differently), was sixty–two when her life was taken from this world. In the first dwelling place of *The Interior Castle*, St. Teresa speaks of our early life when we "don't understand ourselves or know who we are. ... For even though [we] are very involved in the world, [we] have good desires, and sometimes, [we] entrust ourselves to our Lord and reflect on who [we] are." In these first rooms of our life, we "are prevented from seeing the beauty of the castle and from calming down, but [we] have done quite a bit by just having entered." Modern–day mystics begin life building an orientation to God and God's mysteries. The foundation for this orientation is conventional faith, which is followed by a journey to God that goes far beyond the conventional. The spirituality within and around Sister Karen during her early years set the groundwork for her calling and service.

Young Theresa Klimczak was blessed with a faith–filled, supportive family. Her father, John Klimczak, was only eleven years old when he replaced his deceased father in the mines of Wilkes–Barre, Pennsylvania. He worked in the mines so that his blind mother and five sisters could continue living in their company–owned home.

Klimczak Family 1947
Theresa (Sister Karen) – front row, second from left

Her parents, Genevieve (Gen) and John, married and began their own family in the Wilkes–Barre area. However, Sister Karen's mother realized that her family could have a better life away from the mines. She saved enough money for her husband to take a bus to Buffalo, New York. John applied for a job at the Bethlehem Steel Company and was hired the very next day. Soon after, Gen packed up the rest of the family and got a ride with a truck driver who dropped them off in Buffalo. The family settled outside of Buffalo in Lackawanna, New York. Her father's years in the mines and the steel plant would eventually take their toll, plaguing him in later years with complications of Black Lung disease.

Gen and John Klimczak were the parents of twelve children. There were nine brothers: Joseph, William, John, Bernard, Edwin, Raymond, James, Gerald (now deceased), and Robert. There were also three sisters: Mary, Theresa (Sister Karen), and Jean (who became a Franciscan Sister). Sister Karen was their seventh child.

Sister Karen's parents were role models for a life of charity and grace that she would emulate. The Klimczaks joined St. Michael the Archangel parish and always attended Sunday Mass together. The rest of the day was planned around their one o'clock meal, which was a sharing celebration open to all.

Her family's kindness and strength laid the foundation for Sister Karen's ministry. Her sister, Mary Klimczak Lynch, recalls that her parents would help anyone in need, anonymously, so as not to embarrass anyone or make anyone feel indebted.

John Klimczak was inventive and resourceful. He could read a book about building a house and then build one. When land was inexpensive, he joined with three other families to buy 144 acres of land in East Arcade, New York. The families built a small cabin with four bedrooms, one for each family. Theresa and her family spent summers and weekends at the cabin planting vegetable gardens and gathering berries and wild mushrooms. Her father and older brothers also fished and hunted to supplement the food supply for their large family. Sister Jean Klimczak, OSF, Theresa's younger sister, remembers the swing set and the outdoor barbecue her father built for them. She fondly remembers him grilling chicken on that barbecue for the Sunday celebrations. "My parents always reached out to people in need," recalls Sister Jean. "Neighbors and friends would drop in, and it would not be unusual to see twenty–five people gathered at the cabin."

Gen and John with grandchildren at their Arcade cabin

In the tradition of the Klimczak family, Sunday dinners at HOPE House, the halfway house for ex–offenders that Sister Karen would later establish, were open to all and were often a celebration for residents, their families, and guests. Dinner was at one o'clock and, as Sister Karen explained in her journal, *Supper is an opportunity for sharing ... A lot of residents have never experienced a family meal.* Holidays, too, were times of special celebrations at HOPE House: Sister Karen prepared birthday parties, Easter baskets, and Halloween treats for the residents, always remembering the example of charity set by her parents.

When Theresa was young, Halloween took on a special meaning. The Klimczak children would go out and collect as much candy as they could. "Usually we filled two big boxes, but the candy wasn't for us," explains Sister Jean. Her mother and father would take the candy to the poor farm children in East Arcade. "They were very poor–the insulation for their houses was just paper–so we would share what we had with them. It was just a way of life for us."

Theresa liked to read and enjoyed playing baseball with her brothers. She possessed spontaneous creativity and curiosity about everything and everyone around her.

After completing grammar school, Theresa, as well as her two sisters, attended Immaculata Academy in Hamburg, New York. Tuition for the school was $125 a year and bus transportation was another $120. Each of the Klimczak daughters was expected to help earn money toward those costs. Theresa earned most of her school money by babysitting. In her third year of high school, she followed her sister Mary and worked at Our Lady of Victory Infant Home. She was assigned to be a greeter and escort for those visiting the unwed mothers who lived there. She also volunteered her strong secretarial skills in the office of the Infant Home.

Theresa was a dedicated high school student and received honors and recognition for her excellent secretarial skills. During those years, she also continued her passion for reading and her enjoyment of walking. Her sister Mary remembers Theresa walking more than a mile to the public library. Since she was allowed to take out only six books at a time, she walked there often. She took pleasure in being a voracious reader throughout her life.

In 2001, the Immaculata Class of 1961 held its fortieth reunion. Barbara Brennan, one of the organizers, remembers the humor and energy that the former Theresa Klimczak brought to the gathering. Theresa had been such a serious student at Immaculata that many of her former classmates were surprised to see her clown side emerge. Her charismatic joy immediately won the hearts of several women who had remained in touch with each other since high school.

Immaculata 40th class reunion

One of the highlights of the reunion was a game where the players steal a prize away from someone who had already selected it. Barbara remembers Sister Karen going back and forth over a framed copy of the class picture. Barbara started to feel embarrassed that this "poor nun" wasn't getting to keep the picture, but Sister Karen's clown side was just having fun. When Barbara said that she thought Sister Karen should keep the picture, Sister Karen laughed. She was enjoying the game and later reassured Barbara: "Oh, Barb, don't worry. If I wanted, I could make a billion copies of that photo on my computer."

Her comment added to the laughter and endeared Sister Karen to the group.

After the reunion, Barbara Brennan and her two friends, Joyce Meegan and Diane Bialota, invited "Theresa" to join them for their group birthday celebrations. She was also invited to several of Barbara's family parties, especially the annual Christmas gathering. These birthday dinners gave Sister Karen a time to relax and share in discussions of work and family. Sister Karen almost always brought a joke gift to the celebrations, like a rubber chicken that proclaimed, "You're no spring chicken anymore."

The "Theresa" who went to birthday dinners with her friends was the Other Sister Karen, as they called her. She was the "silly self," the Zen clown who needed to relax and share and renew her strength for the next battle against violence.

"Be Truthful, Be Yourself" would prove a lifelong quest for Sister Karen, a journey of prophesy much like the words of Colossians 3:9–10: "You have stripped off the old self with its practices and have clothed yourself with the new self, which is being renewed in knowledge according to the image of its creator."

B*O*UNCE
Others and How We Should Act Toward Others

O stands for "Others and How We Should Act Toward Others." Traditional mystics believe that a vocation to a life of consecration is a profound gift from God and a self–gift in celibacy, poverty, obedience, and fidelity. Sister Karen desired a life of prayer and service. Years later, when she faced major changes in her life and ministry, she would pray for the strength to do what God called her to do. As she states in a journal entry: *Lord, as I reflect on all that is happening, I ask for your confidence, your trust ... Give me the inward confidence that I so often display outwardly.*

In 1962, right after high school, Theresa became a novice with the Franciscan Sisters of Saint Joseph. She wanted to be of service to others and was no doubt attracted to the Franciscan values of integrity, vision, respect, compassion, and service.

Theresa as a postulant

She chose the name "Karen" in honor of her two–year–old niece whose death touched her deeply. Years later, when Sister Karen transferred to the Sisters of St. Joseph, she could have chosen another name, but she kept "Karen."

She attended Immaculata College, which later would be called Hilbert College. In her first year as a novice, she was allowed to take only religious studies and a few liberal arts courses. Sister Edmunette Paczesny, Ph.D., FSSJ, later president emerita of Hilbert, taught several of the education, philosophy, and psychology courses that Sister Karen studied. Sister Edmunette remembers her student's scholarly abilities as well as her outstanding secretarial skills. While Sister Karen was a student, the two of them were responsible for all of the secretarial work for the then college president.

Sister Karen's first teaching assignment was at Most Precious Blood School in Angola, NY. She then taught at St. Stanislaus School in Chicopee, MA. She spent ten years teaching intermediate grades at St. Stanislaus, from 1966 to 1976, and is remembered by her colleagues as a dedicated educator. "She was much loved by children and adults alike during the years she spent here," recalls Sister M. Andrea Ciszewski, FSSJ, superintendent of the Springfield Diocese Catholic Schools. "Her strength was in math and reading," recalls Sister Andrea. "Anyone who observed her knew she was a teacher par excellence. She was very energetic, very creative, and very religious–a woman who wanted to do all she could to assist society."

While teaching in Chicopee, Sister Karen earned her bachelor's degree in education at Westfield State College in Massachusetts. She became an expert in the open–classroom teaching method and used her skills to teach others the technique. After a fire at St. Stanislaus School, she was instrumental in redesigning the new school in the open–classroom learning style. She continued to develop the method and spoke at teachers' conferences and convocations on using the open–

classroom design to improve instruction for all students.

Chicopee alderman William Zaskey, who had been a parish council associate during those years, remembers Sister Karen for her input into the school's design, for her dedication to children and education, and for "wanting to make a pleasant environment for the children."

Sister Karen's love of teaching and creative methodologies would continue through her other assignments at St. Hedwig High School in Detroit, MI, and St. Barnabas and Mount St. Joseph Academy in Buffalo. Her journal entries often reflected her thankfulness for being able to reach out to her students: *I guess I really do enjoy teaching! Lord, I pray that I do some good. I love the kids so much, indeed they are precious ... the kids are so beautiful. I'm enjoying them and life itself. I keep being so grateful for each opportunity you send me. Thanks Lord! Lord, today was so beautiful in school. I've grown to love the students so much. I can't help but realize how much they mean to me!*

In 1978, Sister Karen began her transition to the Congregation of the Sisters of St. Joseph. She was attracted to the community because of its charism, "unity and reconciliation." One way to interpret this charism is "to give another a second chance," which is what Karen's prison ministry came to symbolize.

Transfer to Sisters of St. Joseph
~ 1979 ~

Under the rules of Canon Law at that time, the transfer process from one congregation to another took one year. In the autumn of 1979, Sister Karen completed her transfer at a Mass of celebration when she renewed her vows with the Sisters of St. Joseph. The phrase she chose for the Mass program cover was "Reaching, Risking, Responding to the Spirit of More." These would become the new "three R's" of her future education and life in prison ministry. For one of the readings at the Mass she chose Jeremiah 18:1–6: "I went down to the potter's house and there he was, working at his wheel. Whenever the object of clay which he was making turned out badly in his hand, he tried again, making of the clay another object of whatever sort he pleased."

This representation of God as the potter and us as the clay was a continuing and significant image throughout her ministry. Sister Karen would reflect on this passage many times, as her life began to change and her new work took root. She prepared herself with prayer for the testing that would come and found strength in the passage from Isaiah 48:10: "See, I have refined you like silver, tested you in the furnace of affliction." In 1979, she also received her master's degree in pastoral studies at Loyola University in Chicago.

Sister Karen was a born storyteller. Often, she used personal stories to teach educational and spiritual concepts. Her stories made learning easier, and she saw them as a parallel to Jesus' teachings. *Jesus was a storyteller*, she wrote. *As a creator, He used nature and events of His life to teach others about His Father ... His stories were meant to have an element*

8

of surprise in them. If we reflect on our own lives and the stories that we have experienced that were surprising, were they not moments that we were being touched by the Father.

She would later use this gift of storytelling to teach ex–offenders about God and God's mercy. Sister Karen gave life to some of her storytelling by combining it with her clowning. In this way, she not only shared God's love with children but with adults as well.

By 1984, new opportunities for ministries other than teaching began to present themselves. In May of that year she wrote, *You seem to be calling me Lord, but to what?? Thank you for helping me stay within you. I do love my students so much ... How do I say goodbye ...*

In June she received permission from the Sisters of St. Joseph to join Father Roy Herberger, Sister Mary Pat Barth (another Sister of Saint Joseph), and four college students to form and live in an intentional community. This was a spiritually-based community where members shared responsibilities, resources, and a common vision. For Sister Karen it was important to experience Christian community through laity and religious living together and sharing common values. The small community lived in Father Roy's rectory at Our Lady of Lourdes parish in Buffalo and was based on peace and justice.

Teaching sisters were expected to do a summer service project, so that year Sister Karen chose to go to Providence House in New York City. Providence House was founded in 1979 to provide shelter and support to homeless, formerly incarcerated women and their children. The guiding values of Providence House are hospitality, nonviolence, compassion, and community. Sister Karen would later adopt some of these values at HOPE House. During her summer service at Providence House, she experienced a deep personal transformation as she worked with the women and children. This experience provided an impetus for her future prison ministry.

Sister Karen continued to trust the Lord during this time of change and gained a new vision of her ministry. In a journal entry, she looked at the qualities of Jesus: *Jesus as teacher/friend/leader. Loves–relationship, Understands, Risks, trusts, guides/directs, shares, touches gently, challenges, encourages, models, cares, feels with, reveals himself, allows discovery, supports, healer, awakens giftedness, patient, accepts as is.*

BO<u>U</u>NCE
Use the Gifts God Has Given You

U stands for "Use the Gifts God Has Given You." Sister Karen used her unique gifts throughout her life in service to others. The discernment of how to use her gifts and talent led her to deep meditation and profound prayer. This practice is not unusual for a mystic called to God's work in this world.

Hildegard of Bingen, the twelfth–century German religious visionary, composer, and author, through her deep faith, believed that God is present in all events including our struggles. "On the one hand, your desires and feelings sigh for the narrow path that leads to God," she once advised. "But, on the other hand, you have a whole realm of worries about the people entrusted to you. The former is light; the latter is shadow … . You don't allow yourself to see that they belong together, and this is why you so frequently experience depression in your spirit. For you fail to see your striving for God and your concern for people as a unity" (Durka 1991).

On the first day of 1985, after her work at Providence House, Sister Karen embarked on a new calling, a ministry to ex–offenders. She shared her joy and thanksgiving at this time in her journal: *Well, Lord in this new year I ask for the gift of sharing my prayer, my faith, more confidently with others. Help me to relax in you, to speak knowing you will place the words on my lips. The gift of gentleness and strength to reach out to those imprisoned – I know you are with me in all of this.*

It was then that the necessary work of establishing a home for ex–offenders began. Sister Karen continued her teaching duties and with the help of Father Roy Herberger, her mentor and friend, established HOPE House, a communal home for nonviolent ex–offenders. She was encouraged by her religious community's approval of the project but saddened by the negative view some people shared about this new venture. She prayed, *Cry out to God in prayer … Be with me–I have been so accepted by you–by the SSJs–by this parish–by a confidence in me as I reach out to these ex–offenders.*

It was her interest in words and their meanings as well as a love of acronyms that influenced its naming: HOPE House would stand for Home Of Positive Experience. An earlier idea for the meaning of the letters was broader: *H stood for Help not a hindrance; O was for Optimism, P was for Person–centered, not prison–producing; and E was for Experiences.*

The initial goals for HOPE, Inc. had specific objectives that included Worker's Goals, Educational Aspects, and Extension to Others. Sister Karen envisioned HOPE House as a "faith–sharing community." Her prayer was that it would become the broader "common unity" she believed could emerge from the narrower concept of just "community."

HOPE House would have rules, and these rules would be modified as the need arose. Rules would help to keep unity in the house and help to change ingrained negative behaviors of the residents. Sister Karen knew the survival of this ministry depended on a strict schedule and house rules. Many times she had to forgive the residents who broke the rules and went back to drugs or alcohol. These disappointments taught her forgiveness. She often told others how "her guys" challenged her to really live the Gospel, to see how forgiving or how loving she could truly be.

At the time HOPE House began, a diocesan priest named Father Joseph Bissonette was also active in human rights and nonviolence work. The paths of Sister Karen and Father Bissonette crossed often, and he left a lasting impression on her. In 1987 Father Bissonette was murdered in St. Bartholomew parish rectory. Only two weeks after his death, Monsignor David P. Herlihy was also murdered on Buffalo's East Side in the rectory of St. Matthew Church. The same two young men would be convicted of both murders.

Two years after the murder of Father Bissonette, Sister Karen moved HOPE House into his former rectory. She converted the room in which he was killed into a prayer room where she would begin every morning in prayer with the residents. Sister Karen stated in an interview, "Father Joe Bissonette reached out to the poor, to the forgotten of society. ... He is the inspiration for the men and staff at the house." This description of the prayer room is posted on the HOPE House web site: "The very room where Father Joe died is a place where nine ex–offenders (Christian, Muslim, Jew, Native American) and Sister Karen Klimczak (a Sister of St. Joseph) join hands in prayer–lives are changed, men are reborn and given a new chance in life."

In 1991 Sister Karen stopped teaching and devoted herself fulltime to the HOPE House ministry. In memory of Father Joe, HOPE House was renamed Bissonette House in 2003. For Sister Karen, work with former inmates was a way of living the Gospel. These men were outward signs of her intrinsic belief in the need for forgiveness and healing that was a driving force in her life.

In addition to her work at Bissonette House, Sister Karen was part of a committee that worked on bringing together Bud Welch, whose daughter Julie was among the 167 people killed in the 1995 bombing of the Oklahoma City Federal Building, and Bill McVeigh, father of Timothy McVeigh who was executed for that crime. Because the challenge of forgiveness is central to living the Gospels, Sister Karen and Father Herberger visited prison to offer forgiveness to the murderers of Father Bissonette and Monsignor Herlihy.

Sister Karen believed that both words and actions have the power to bring about change. She had a simple explanation for her mission and calling. "I always wanted to do something for victims. I always wanted to do something against violence in the city ... and I will do everything I can do in my small way to create a more nonviolent society" (Daybreak, 2007).

Her message of nonviolence is spreading not only throughout the city but everywhere people hear her story. She has become a true apostle for peace. People from the community clearly recognize and witness to Sister Karen's powerful dedication.

"Tireless and in near constant motion," that is how Rev. Matthew Brown, pastor at the Pentecostal Temple Church of God in Christ, described Sister Karen. "In Western New York, they called her Mother Teresa in fast forward. Without a trace of hyperbole, they called her a gift from God."

11

Paula Voell, a columnist for *The Buffalo News*, gives us an insider's view of Sister Karen in this description posted on the Internet:

> Most clearly, I remember wondering how a person so diminutive could be so powerful. I saw her at a prayer meeting with a circle of men, each one towering over her. It surprised me to see her referred to as 5 feet, 6 inches tall; my recollection is of a tiny person. In fact, one person I interviewed called her a "little peanut of a woman."
>
> I thought of her as a mighty mite: someone who knew what she wanted to do and went after it. Maybe her spunkiness came from growing up with nine brothers. Besides that, she was humble, a person who might go unnoticed. (*The Buffalo News*, 2006)

Edward Dennis of the Cephas prison ministry described her this way: "Any person like that who tries to help anybody in need, is from God. I hope we find more people like her. They'll never match her. But at least they'll walk in her footsteps, and keep the light shining."

In her ministry, she followed a simple path, trying to give the parolees what they needed–attention, community, and rules. "She accepted everybody. She always gave them a second chance." This is how Sister Mary Johnice Rzadkiewicz, CSSF, who directs the Response to Love Center in Buffalo, described Sister Karen. "She wasn't afraid. When you live amongst the people, you drop your fears. She was forgiving and that's probably how she would be toward her accused killer. She died for peace."

BOU**N**CE
Never Hurt Anyone

N stands for "Never Hurt Anyone." It could easily stand for "Nonviolence," as Sister Karen devoted her life to bringing this message to others.

Sister Karen spent much of her life praying for self–awareness as a means of developing awareness of others as she prepared to minister to ex–offenders, victims of violence, and their families.

Anthony de Mello, SJ, author and, until his death, director of the Sadhana Institute for Pastoral Studies in Poona, India, explains that when we are attuned to our own feelings, we are more aware of the feelings of others. When we are aware of our reactions to others, we are able "to go out to them in love, without doing any harm":

> Some of the great mystics tell us that when they reach the stage of illumination they become mysteriously filled with a sense of deep reverence. Reverence for God, reverence for life in all its forms … it is as if even things have become persons to them–and as a result of this, their respect and love for persons become heightened. (de Mello, 1978)

Sister Karen's love and respect for the individual and her abiding faith in God helped her create a legacy of programs and good works that spread a gospel of caring and nonviolence. "Her legacy," explains Father Herberger, "is one of humility, service, encouragement, and peace. The best way to remember her is through forgiveness."

"Karen challenged all of us to have a deep relationship with God and each other," adds Sister Jean Klimczak. This relationship especially extended to prisoners and ex–offenders.

"She felt they were forgotten," Mary Klimczak Lynch says. "She felt they never had a chance unless somebody was there to help them."

Sister Karen also believed in the power of testimonials or life stories. To her, they were another form of storytelling. Sister Karen prefaced her storytelling with this background about the men whom she served: "When a person is released from a New York State correctional facility, he is given $40 and a bus ticket. Many have absolutely no possessions, only the clothes they are wearing. HOPE House is an opportunity for each of the men to begin life anew!" The following real–life stories, as well as others that she liked to tell, can be found on the Hope of Buffalo web site.

13

The Birthday Party

It was Dan's twenty–seventh birthday, and we celebrated with a party.

We enjoy celebrations! We had a cake with candles and ice cream and a small present.

As we began to sing, I looked over at Dan and saw tears coming down his cheeks. I went over to Dan and whispered, 'What's wrong?'

He said, "I've never had a birthday party before."

The Sofa

Joe had just moved into an apartment and called me asking if we had a sofa he could use. He explained he would use it to sleep on and also to sit on, especially when someone came by to visit him. A group of us were in our TV room where we had two sofas.

I said to the men, "We can give Joe one of these sofas."

David remarked, "But, Karen, we always use it."

My comment was, "Don't worry. God will provide."

David just rolled his eyes back as if to say, "Here she goes again!" The men took the sofa out to the van to deliver it to Joe and when they were coming back for directions, the phone was ringing.

I answered it and then responded to the person, "Yes, we certainly could use a sofa" and took the donor's address down.

When I hung up the phone, David said, "God works fast, doesn't he?"

Testimonials about Sister Karen
by Former Residents of HOPE House/Bissonette House

Kevin came back often as a volunteer to help Sister Karen. "She was a very powerful woman in her walk and the things she did and the things she stood for," he remembers. "She was a small person, but she exuded so much confidence and power that she did have a lot of respect."

"She was a ball of fire. I mean a real ball of fire," comments Roger Weisser. "She had so much energy it was unbelievable ... It takes a special person to walk in those shoes. You could be with her for ten minutes, and you knew she was a special person."

Willie White lived at Bissonette House for six months after his parole. Then he worked as a counselor for other men who had recently left prison. He would return regularly to help with work around Bissonette House. Willie says of Sister Karen: "She helped me in every way, any way she could. She was like a mother to us. I wondered how she could take care of all of us, but she had a big heart. She gave me the chance I needed to keep out of [prison], and I haven't been back since. There are a lot of us who did make it, who see the impact she had on us."

"She was a person that could look at sorrow, pain, and despair in a person and tell them that they are somebody and they can be someone," explains Juan Flores. "I was able to turn my life around because she showed me what courage was. She was just all over the place and such a bundle of joy. I asked her, 'Where do you get this energy?' And she said, 'I just love what I do.' She's a fine example of what I would strive to be. We're very fortunate to have had such a servant amongst us."

Bob Marts echoes those words of praise: "She's like the Mother Antonia of prison ministry. She was such an inspiration. If more people would look at her, and look at what she was able to accomplish, just because of her heart, and how many lives she actually touched and changed, they'd actually realize they can do the same."

Doug shares that he wrote Sister Karen a letter while he was in prison, and she came to visit him. Then she invited him to live at HOPE House. In return, Doug wants to lead a life that would make Sister Karen proud of him. "She understood I was a father, and I had young kids at the time. She gave me the direction I needed in my life. She explained I needed to go to meetings, I needed to attend counseling, and I needed to find work. With all of that, she helped me every step of the way."

Cliff Zane knew from the start that Sister Karen "had a warm heart. She would give you the shirt off her back if it was the last thing she could give you. She would sit down and talk to you. She wasn't afraid. There are very few people in this world that will look at you and look at you as a person. She was one of them."

Jim Bruckman adds, "I did almost three decades of incarceration, and when I first met her, I was sad, bitter. She said, 'What are you so sad and bitter about?' I didn't think I could make it out here, but she said, 'If you survived three decades in prison, it's a piece of cake out here.' And she was right. She always gave you hope. She hit me in my heart, and made me feel special. … Inside [prison] is a world of violence. And she was just a woman of peace. And I will survive because of her."

Sister Karen knew that with the grace of God she could make a difference in these men's lives. Many of the former residents would invite her to their weddings or ask her to be godmother to their children. She also ministered to sick and dying ex–offenders to whom she brought comfort and hope.

When Sister Karen was murdered, sadness and shock reverberated throughout Buffalo and all across the country. Sister Mary Anne Butler, SSJ, in ongoing correspondence with an inmate named Scotty at the California Men's State Prison in San Luis Obispo, had told him all about Sister Karen and the Bissonette House program. Shortly after Sister Karen's death, a package arrived for Sister Mary Anne. It contained a large hand–illustrated card, along with twenty–seven heartfelt comments, such as the following, written by inmates who felt they "knew" Sister Karen:

Sister Karen, from one world to the next, beauty will always follow.

Dave

* * *

When God saw his wonderful servant harmed, thunderclouds went out and covered the mountain. Beautiful Sister, to God you have returned.

Thank you for all you do for us prisoners. God Bless Your Spirit, Sister.

Buffalo,
Cherokee Nation

* * *

Sister Karen SSJ, you were a shining light to us. Especially those of us on the other side. "May you sleep with God."

Love and Prayers,
Benny G.

* * *

Sister Mary Anne, words alone can't and won't be able to express how much I'll miss Sister Karen. She was a Saint in my eyes. She worked with ex–convicts and gave Peace and Love to these people. Whoever she came in contact with she did show them Love! Sister Karen will always live in my heart! Just know that Sister Karen is in heaven with God. I send each of you Sisters a Hug!

Love always,
Scotty

For Sister Karen the dove was a visual and spiritual symbol of peace. It was her passion to bring peace to the hearts of the residents of her halfway house and to those in the community touched by violence. The dove represented not only nonviolence but also the peace of the Lord.

In establishing a Remembering and Pledging service, creating the "NONVIOLENCE begins with ME!" signs and smaller doves for prayer vigils, and posting a huge dove in front of Bissonette House that kept count of the number of days since the last homicide in Buffalo, Sister Karen truly became Buffalo's "Apostle of Nonviolence."

Sister Karen's peace dove signs were a reflection of what Joan Chittister, OSB, author and national and international lecturer, describes in her book, *Wisdom Distilled From the Daily* (1990). "It is not that Peace is just the absence of conflict or control by force. Peace comes from trying over and over again to find our place in the universe without violence, without selfishness, without demands."

BOUN*C*E

Be a Caring Person

C The letter C in Bounce stands for "Be a Caring Person." Sister Karen spent her life caring for the "*anawim*," the poor in spirit, the disenfranchised, the marginal or, literally translated from Hebrew, the remnants of society. She lived with the *anawim* and ministered to them, and her vocation and commitment grew and multiplied. Sister Karen's passion and compassion are both recognizable signs of mysticism:

> The true fire–in–the–belly mystic has such passion that it occupies not only [her] daytime work but [her] nighttime dreams. [She] lives and breathes this passion as a form of dedication to God and humanity. [Her] charisma and effectiveness stem from humility, and [she] leaves a lasting impression on those that [she] touches."
> (Borysenko, 1997)

In an article in the local newspaper, Rev. Matthew L. Brown, pastor of the Pentecostal Temple Church of God in Christ, gave this visual description of Sister Karen's passion at work:

> Sister Karen Klimczak moved quick as the wind off Lake Erie. A peace–loving nun who crisscrossed the city with such speed that friends wondered, only half–jokingly, if she hadn't borrowed some Catholic saint's miraculous ability to bilocate. In a day she might race from counseling ex–offenders at the halfway house she ran, to praying at a murder victim's vigil, then head to the youth center she founded before donning a clown suit and bouncing joyously through a senior center. (*The Buffalo News,* 2006)

Sister Karen was involved not only with her work at Bissonette House; she also started several outreach projects and continued her peace dove campaign for nonviolence. She was a dedicated supporter of P.E.A.C.E. (Parents Encouraging Accountability and Closure for Everyone). With P.E.A.C.E. members she continued her dedication to prayer vigils for victims and reached out to families traumatized by homicide.

Yolanda Freeman was grieving over the news that her son Michael had been murdered. She remembers Sister Karen coming to her home with a peace dove in her hand. "It made me feel loved," Yolanda said. "For someone who didn't know me, to share time with my family in our time of loss."

Sister Karen was a visible sign of God's love and peace during these times of violence and loss. "Almost every time I was sent out to the scene of a homicide, Sister Karen Klimczak would be there," remembers Lynn Dixon, a reporter for the local television station WGRZ–TV:

> If I was doing a follow–up story the next day, Sister Karen would be walking through the neighborhood, without fear, in her trademark tee–shirt, jeans, and sneakers.... I headed out to an east side neighborhood the morning after a young man was gunned down. The crime tape had come down, and the homicide detectives were finishing up their work going door to door.

We were advised to "be careful," and led to the home of a grieving family. In no time, Sister Karen appeared at the house ministering to the relatives. She took hold of their hands, formed a prayer circle, and began praying for the murder victim, for the suspect, and for the family and friends. Later, she started handing out flyers, notifying residents of a prayer vigil.

A couple of months later, I was again following up on a homicide … and in a scene that had become commonplace, I turned to see Sister Karen walking through the neighborhood with flyers, notifying residents of a prayer vigil to honor the life of a murder victim and to pray for peace. Later she turned up at the home of the victim's family with a cutout dove she placed on the family's front lawn.

Sister Karen was unyielding in her quest for peace and undaunted by the threats that may have existed around her.

Sister Karen was inspired to further the message of the nonviolence peace signs. She created new dove–shaped signs that read: "I Leave PEACEPRINTS." She explained that a "peaceprint" was as unique as a footprint in the snow or a fingerprint at a crime scene. She hoped her peaceprint signs would encourage others to seek peace through acts of love and kindness. This would be her greatest legacy. The SSJ Sister Karen Klimczak Center for Nonviolence web site explains: "Each hopeful sign is evidence that Sister Karen's life held a deeper meaning, a commitment for all people to live nonviolently."

Sister Karen worked on the dove–shaped signs with her friend Sister Rosalind Rosolowski, CSSF, chaplain at Attica Correctional Facility. Sister Karen ordered two thousand signs that were then cut out by inmates at the facility. All of the signs were ready by the end of March 2006, but, rather than wait until the July "Pledging and Remembering" service to distribute them, she considered ways to introduce the peaceprint signs sooner, on some relevant date or occasion. Little did anyone imagine that that occasion would be her funeral.

"It was as if she were saying," Sister Roz recalls, "'Now that I have left you, I leave peaceprints.' If you know you are doing what you are supposed to be doing and where and with whom, that eliminates a lot of fear. The grace of God works within you. I believe there is a tremendous love that overcomes fear and that's what operated in Karen's life. She had tremendous love and belief in what she was doing."

Rev. Kenyatta T. Cobb, chaplain of the Buffalo Police Department, describes Sister Karen in this way:

Who is this little nun? She's the moral conscience of Buffalo. She's an agent of spiritual good. … She crossed a line where her faith became more important than her life. … You serve because of the love of God that has been put in you.
(*The Buffalo News*, 2006)

The personification of the letter "C" in Bounce is seen in Sister Karen's life lived as a "Caring Person," in her concern for all, and in her creative outreach activities.

In the song "Peaceprints," which he wrote, David F. Granville captures her caring spirit and ongoing work for peace: "Walk with me, fly with me, follow the way of love. See the path unfolding now, led on by a Dove. Hearing God we live in trust, listen to the sound. People singing, people praying, ways of peace abound."

BOUNC*E*

Every Person Is Special

"Every Person Is Special" is the most important lesson of Sister Karen Klimczak's life. It is her life's prayer in her journey of faith. This message is made meaningful in the words of a Canisius High School student who, after taking a tour of the Bissonette House, said, "Sister Karen taught us that you cannot judge people by their past."

"Giving people a second chance" was the driving force of her HOPE House ministries and her work for nonviolence. Sister Karen's journey as a contemporary mystic allowed her to be the love of God for others, often the outcasts, the broken and hurting. She was God's goodness and light to those who longed for compassion and, like traditional mystics, this love and light of God often lifted her spirit to ecstasy. Yet we can only surmise how on that Good Friday, April 14, 2006, Sister Karen experienced the pain of disappointment and regret. She may have felt an overwhelming sadness that the God Love she tried to channel to one of "her guys" had not touched him yet.

Earlier on Good Friday afternoon, Sister Karen joined other participants in downtown Buffalo for the Stations of the Cross. Around her neck, she wore a white wooden cross that bore the name of a person murdered in Buffalo that year. Later that evening, parishioners of SS. Columba–Brigid Church, where Sister Karen was the pastoral associate, remembered seeing her for the last time after the 7 p.m. Good Friday service. She returned to Bissonette House around 9 p.m. and shortly thereafter was on the third floor talking to Robert Walker, a resident at the house.

He remembers her mentioning Craig Lynch, the newest resident, who had been out of prison for only nine days. She felt that Craig was ready for a fresh start, and she told Robert that on Holy Thursday Craig had helped her put strings on the wooden crosses for the Stations of the Cross walk. "I think Craig's doing well. I think he's going to be all right," Sister Karen had remarked. Then she locked the side door and went to her room.

According to Sister Karen's family and friends, she neither lived in fear nor was cavalier about the potential dangers that accompanied her work. She kept a cautious safety routine and was never reckless. On Holy Saturday afternoon, she uncharacteristically missed several appointments.

Holy Saturday night, after she did not show up for the Easter Vigil Mass at her parish, Father Roy Herberger and Sister Karen's brother went to Bissonette House. They searched for her throughout the house and the surrounding area. Robert Walker, the resident she had spoken to the night before, phoned police and reported her missing. The police investigators working on the case warned that her disappearance was very suspicious, and they feared foul play.

Bishop Edward Kmiec of Buffalo released an official statement Easter Sunday:

> We are praying that Sister Karen is safe and will soon be home. She is a woman of God who has selflessly given spiritual guidance and her time to many of those who have been cast off by society. On this Easter Sunday, the day of the Lord's resurrection, I ask that everyone in Western New York join me in praying for

Sister Karen's safety. She remains in our thoughts along with her family, friends, and the Sisters of St. Joseph.

Sister Jean Klimczak, whose ministry at the time was in Olean, New York, received a symbolic message at a sunrise Easter Mass that Sunday. It was a beautiful, bright morning with no clouds in sight. During the homily, she was attracted to a bright silver plane in the sky. The plane was traveling from east to west and suddenly made a right–angle turn and disappeared into the blue. Words suddenly came into her mind. "Someone that you know very well is journeying into God."

Sister Jean immediately asked if something would happen to her sister Mary. "Will her cancer come back?" The answer she received was "No." Then she thought of her upcoming trip to Brazil. "Will something happen to me on the way to Brazil?" she asked. Again the answer was "No." Then she heard the words, "You don't understand."

When she returned to St. Mary's office, a phone call awaited her. Although she and Sister Karen called each other every Sunday, this call was from her other sister, Mary, who told her that Karen was missing. In her heart she knew that Karen was not missing but had died and was now journeying into God. She knew her sister had indeed gone home.

The initial search on Easter Sunday by parishioners of SS. Columba–Brigid Church found articles of Sister Karen's clothing in a dumpster at the corner of Grider Street and Delavan Avenue. On Easter Monday, an entire city hoped and prayed. More than one hundred people set out in a yard–to–yard search for her. Groups of six or seven, accompanied by a police officer, hunted through backyards and alleys of the neighborhood surrounding Bissonette House. Also on Easter Monday the nine residents of Bissonette House were interviewed and given drug tests. Only Craig Lynch tested positive. At first, he claimed he knew nothing about Sister Karen's disappearance, but late Monday afternoon he finally confessed to killing her. He led police to Sister Karen's body which was buried in a shallow grave inside a shed, a few miles from Bissonette House.

Two prayer vigils were held for Sister Karen that Monday evening. One took place at St. Elizabeth Motherhouse in Allegany, New York [where Sister Jean's Franciscan community is based]. The other was at Ephesus Cathedral, next door to Bissonette House. Before the vigils began, Sister Karen's family, the Bissonette House board of directors, and her close friends were notified by police that they had found Sister Karen's body. Others in the community were still unaware of this terrible loss.

Craig Lynch insisted the murder was an accident. According to his confession, he passed Sister Karen's room and saw her cell phone by her computer. He went in to steal the cell phone to sell for drug money. Hearing her coming, he hid behind the door. Sister Karen walked in on him. Her autopsy showed death was caused by manual suffocation and blunt force trauma.

This act of violence began an eerie parallel to the Easter story. Craig Lynch took Sister Karen's body from Bissonette House, drove a few miles, and hid her near his mother's house. He then left and sold her cell phone "on the street" for what turned out to be fake cocaine. He returned to his mother's house in the early hours of Holy Saturday morning and took Sister Karen's body across the street to a shed behind an abandoned house. After digging a hole in the dirt floor inside the shed and saying a prayer, he buried her.

After Lynch confessed, police investigated the crime scene and removed Sister Karen's body. The crime scene was cleared, and a reporter's observations were posted on the Internet:

> Slivers of sunlight poured through the patchy roof of the crumbling shed, revealing the hole that had held Sister Karen's body for three long days. Rusty paint cans, brown hiking boots, an old mattress, and piles of dirt surrounded the grave. At the bottom of the hole, someone had left a paper cut–out of a white dove, an apparent tribute to Sister Karen's devotion to peace. (Posting Goddess Web Log, 2006)

An entire city wept, and two thousand mourners filled St. Ann Church for Sister Karen's funeral. People came from all over to celebrate her life–people who knew her as a sibling, as a friend, or as a colleague; people who did not know her at all but knew of her life, her work, and her death. Sister Karen had discussed with her sisters Mary and Jean what to do if anything happened to her. She wanted one white dove released at her funeral. As people outside St. Ann Church watched, a single white dove was released, flew up in what seemed a perfectly straight line, and suddenly turned east into the clouds.

Bishop Edward Kmiec issued another formal statement regarding Sister Karen's death:

> I am deeply saddened by the death of Sister Karen Klimczak. She was a woman of peace, and like so many before her, gave her life in service to her God, her Church, and the community she loved. We will be forever grateful for the many gifts that Sister Karen shared with others, and we must make sure that her work continues, for it is people like Sister Karen who devote their lives, often at great peril, to assist those in society who so desperately need help, compassion, and understanding.

"If one word would be synonymous with Karen," explained Father Roy Herberger, "it would be 'forgive'... and she would be saying that about Craig. She would be the first person to say, 'Father, forgive him; he really doesn't know what he's doing.'"

Rev. Matthew Brown of the Pentecostal Temple Church of God in Christ also makes a correlation between Sister Karen's work and the Word of God:

> Sister Karen's legacy is that of the crux of Christianity, the purpose of Jesus and the fulfillment of the scripture: 'Greater love hath no man than this: that a man would lay down his life for a friend.' The timing of this betrayal, murder, mishap, and tragic event was prophetically in sync with another historical betrayal that by divine design completed God's plan for redemption for humanity. My faith causes me to believe that people will not die until they have fulfilled their purpose or the opportunity of that purpose has expired. Sister Karen's life assignment and purpose had wonderful fulfillment ... Sister Karen, like Nehemiah, responded to

the plight of those she loved. Her saintly compassion and life purpose caused her to repair the 'broken walls' of their lives through daily acts of kindness and consistent affirmation of their humanity. Like Jesus, Sister Karen's Judas was a betrayer of kindness, who through his own life choices impacted a region by selfishly taking a life without right. Sister Karen would want us to extend this 'peace–breaker' and others who kill with reckless abandon the grace of the risen Christ. She advocated nonviolence and believed in reconciliation from the root of love, not retaliation. The hundreds of lives she impacted, along with the thousands of families she touched, must become the 'new army of compassion' and complete her mission of peace and reconciliation. (*The Buffalo News,* 2006)

Prior to Craig Lynch's sentencing, Sister Jean Klimczak addressed the courtroom and read from a prophetic 1991 entry in Sister Karen's journal that spoke directly to the person who might do her harm and offered him forgiveness. *"I forgive you for what you have done and I will always watch over you, help you in whatever way I can."*

At the sentencing, Judge Sheila DiTullio had to press Craig Lynch several times to apologize to Sister Karen's family. He was sentenced to twenty–five years to life in prison. Judge DiTullio added these remarks:

You killed an exceptional woman. Sister Karen truly believed in the mission that parolees can turn their lives around. You let Sister Karen down, and I don't need to tell you that. Her life was a very clear statement day after day. Sister Karen's murder has marked each of us in ways we will know forever. I hope that our choices and lives will leave peaceprints around the world.

After the sentencing, Sister Jean commented, "Karen was a person who witnessed peace. She was a witness of forgiveness, and she challenges us to be witnesses of peace and forgiveness." The Klimczak family had forgiven Craig Lynch and felt it was time to carry on Sister Karen's mission of peace. Sister Jean explained, "She taught me to accept what is." Certainly all the men at Bissonette House were not success stories, but Sister Karen took joy in all that she could do for each of them. Perhaps she knew that one would disappoint her more than the others, but she also knew that forgiveness was the way to God.

It is Sister Karen's deep sense of purpose to serve God that will always be remembered. Her work continues to live on, especially in her peaceprint doves visible in yards and windows all over Western New York. Within months of her death, four thousand more signs were distributed. The "I Leave PEACEPRINTS" signs are reminders for all in the Western New York area and for people across the country to work for nonviolence and to continue Sister Karen's ministries.

The SSJ Sister Karen Klimczak Center for Nonviolence has been established by the Sisters of St. Joseph. Initially organized by SSJ Associates Audrey and Jim Mang, the Center's mission is to carry on Sister Karen's vision for a world without violence. Sister Karen's mystic journey was lighted by a vision of replacing violence with God's love. She took that living peace everywhere she went. She best defined her work and her life in a video interview for the Diocese of Buffalo:

> I found myself called to really be here with the guys at HOPE House. HOPE isn't [just] for men who have been incarcerated. Hope is for me to grow, to see brokenness in eyes and hearts of individuals. When the brokenness is there, we can see God, and God becomes real. And he has become more real for me through HOPE than any other experience I have had. I believe I am truly living a religious life as I think a religious life should be lived.

JOAN ALBARELLA, professor emerita at the University of Buffalo Educational Opportunity Center, is author of several mystery novels, poetry books, articles, and short stories, an editor of A Journey of Light In Darkness *by Sister Judith Fenyvesi, SSS, and editor of* The Abandoned Poor *by John DiBiase, MSW.*

KAREN WHITNEY is a University of Buffalo emerita having served as a technical writer and registrar at the Educational Opportunity Center. She is the author of published articles and short stories.

References

Apostle of Peace. 2007. Daybreak TV Productions. Buffalo, NY.

Borysenko, Joan. 1997. *7 Paths to God.* Carlsbad, CA: Hay House, Inc.

Carrubba, Sandy McPherson. 1995. A place of new beginnings. *St. Anthony Messenger.* (March):15–16.

Chittister, Joan, OSB. 1990. *Wisdom Distilled From The Daily*, New York: Harper & Row.

Ciemcioch, Mark. 2007. Craig Lynch gets 25 years to life for murder of Sister Karen. *Western New York Catholic* (April).

de Mello, Anthony, SJ. 1978. *Sadhana: A Way to God.* New York: Bantam Doubleday Dell.

Dixon, Lynn. April 19, 2006. Memories of Sister Karen Klimczak. http://www.wgrz.com/news/columnist/blogs/2 The Newsroom – article aspx?storqid=3724 (accessed July 2007).

Jarvis, Thea. 1981. Colorful clowning at Camp Promise. Included with permission of *The Georgia Bulletin*, Archdiocese of Atlanta, http://.georgiabulletin.org/local/1981/08/06/al (accessed July 19, 2007).

Other Sources

Buechi, Patrick J. Sister Karen Klimczak remembered one year after her death. Western New York Catholic (April 2007).

Durka, Gloria. Praying With Hildegard of Bingen, Winona, MN: St. Mary's Press, 1991.

Ellis, Lee. 2002–2003. Who are the anawim? http://www.leellis.com/anawim.html (accessed July 2007).

Hopeministries, pg. 5. html:http://www.hopeofBuffalo.org/ (accessed July 14, 2007).

Hope of Buffalo, Inc. http://www.wnyreligion.net/pp. 2–6 (accessed July 7, 2007.)

Lane, Belden C. October 1989. Merton as Zen clown. Theology Today: 46. http://Theologytoday. ptsem.edu/oct1989/v46–3article/htm (accessed July 2007).

Miller, Anna. February 20, 2007. Sister Karen's legacy lives on in center for nonviolence. http:// sisterkarencenter.org/index_files/page382.htm (accessed July 2007).

Posting Goddess Web Log. April 18, 2006. http://www.buffalonews.com/editorial/ 20060418/1027885.asp (accessed July 2007).

Posting Goddess Web Log. April 19, 2006. http://www.wivb.com/global/story/asp?S=47.V= menu41_9_19_3 (accessed July 2007).

Posting Goddess Web Log (April 20, 2006) http://www.buffalonews.com/editorial/ 20060420/1043198,asp (accessed July 2007).

Resspeaks.htm. http://www.hopeofbuffalo.org/mission.htm (accessed August 6, 2007).

Sister Karen Klimczak, SSJ, disciple of peace is murdered. http://www.buffalodiocese.org/ stories/ sr_klimczak.htm (accessed July 7, 2007).

Sister Karen Klimczak, Missing, April 2006, N.Y. http://fromwisperstor.6.forumer.com /a/sister_ Karen_Klimczak_Missing_April 2006_NY_pos (accessed July 7, 2007).

Staba, David. Sister Karen's hopeful legacy lives on. http://www.hopeofbuffalo.org/sisterkaren.htm (accessed August 6, 2007).

Welch, John. Spiritual Pilgrims, New York: Paulist Press, 1982.

Welcome to Providence House. http://www.providencehouse.org/ (accessed August 8, 2007).

Young, Robyn. Remembering Sister Karen. http://hopeofbufffalo.org/Remembering_sister_karen_ watch.htm (accessed July 7, 2007).

I leave
PEACEPRINTS

Sr. Karen Klimczak SSJ
10-27-43 to 4-14-06

Non-Violence Begins
With Me

Our Friendship and Her Ministry

Margaret McAloon, M.D.

Walk with me, fly with me, follow the way of love.
See the path unfolding now, led on by a Dove ...
(From "Peaceprints" song by David F. Granville)

~ Our Lady of Lourdes ~

My friendship with Karen and her prison ministry intertwined in many ways. We met in 1981, shortly after I moved to Buffalo to join the department of medicine at State University of New York at Buffalo. I was looking for a church and joined Our Lady of Lourdes. The humanity of that place drew me inside and changed many of my stereotypes. I developed close relationships with the people in the parish, and it was at Lourdes that I met Karen. I remember a snowy day when we were cleaning the church, and afterwards, Father Roy, Karen, and some of the students she was living with went to the Anchor Bar. It was the first time I really talked with Karen. She and Father Roy were involved with prison ministry and encouraged me to participate. I started to write to and visit a woman prisoner from Texas who had no contact with anyone on the outside. With that, Karen and I had more in common.

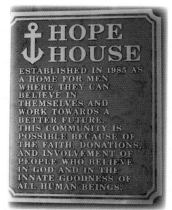

Plaque on Bissonette House that was originally HOPE House

~ HOPE House ~

A few years later, Karen began talking about setting up a halfway house for released prisoners to be called HOPE House. She knew God called her to do this ministry, and she was going forward to establish it, no matter what happened. Karen was down–to–earth and dedicated, but she was like a bull in a china shop. She would be 110 percent involved in whatever she was doing. In 1985 Karen's first HOPE House was established in the vacant Transfiguration convent. Her motto was *HOPE is not a way out ... but a way through.* The acronym stands for: *H* for Help not a hindrance; *O* for Optimism; *P* for Person–centered, not prison–producing; and *E* for Experiences. She tried to make the goals for HOPE comprehensive enough to cover the needs of ex–offenders and those still in prison and also educate people in the community.

In a journal entry, Karen translated the goals into a place where the men would first and foremost experience HOPE as a home:

1) *A home where men can find a loving, caring, and supportive Christian community and atmosphere.*

2) *A place to call 'home' – where sharing is an integral part of the lifestyle; sharing in the home setting, meals, option for praying together, a place of encouragement.*

3) *Someone present at home at all times.*

4) *Take advantage of soup kitchen for lunch, breakfast on own, supper meal together.*

Hope House, circa 1987

~ *Karen and Father Joe Bissonette* ~

Transfiguration convent didn't work out. It was just too big, not like a home and that was her first priority. We continued to look for the right setting but often ran into difficulty with zoning boards. Then in 1987, Father Joe Bissonette was murdered in the rectory of St. Bartholomew Church. Eventually the rectory was available to buy. It couldn't be a more perfect location for Karen's HOPE House. The neighbors, however, on and around Grider Street were resistant. Karen visited them, door–to–door, and very carefully addressed their fears. She "schmoozed" them. Father Bissonette's sister Joanne publicly supported Karen at a neighborhood meeting saying that her brother would want HOPE House, and Joanne's comments made all the difference. The neighbors were won over, and HOPE House relocated to Grider Street. Karen remembered the words her friend Father Joe once said to her: "If ever I can do anything for you, just let me know." She felt he had been instrumental in obtaining this sacred place.

Karen was devoted to Father Joe Bissonette's spirit and did everything to promote his memory. She dedicated a garden to him, named it "Peace Park," and added a large monument engraved with Father Joe's image and his message, "Teach us how to live, God of Love Forgive! Forgive!"

Photo – George Schaeffer

Father Joe Bissonette marker in Peace Park

29

When you walk into the house, a large portrait of Father Joe welcomes each person and is a constant reminder to the guys that a great witness to Jesus' life once lived there. Everywhere you look in the house, Father Joe is remembered. In the room where he was murdered, Karen held prayer services with the guys. On the wall hangs a beautiful artwork depicting Father Joe doing the corporal works of mercy. Whenever Karen would give talks, her message always included the work and spirit of Father Joe. She was determined to keep his name alive. When things were not going well, she would ask Joe to help, and inevitably her prayers were answered. He was her inspiration. Eventually, she renamed the house "Bissonette House," to once again honor Father Joe.

~ *Karen and Penn* ~

Margaret, Becky, Penn and Karen at Becky's First Communion

During those first years of HOPE House, I met my husband, fell in love, and married. It was a small wedding with only thirty–six people, including Karen and Father Roy. Karen was exuberant, she was fun, she laughed. She wasn't always serious. My husband Penn was a college professor of business who became an EMT paramedic–his "midlife crisis." As time went on, Karen gave Penn the courage to expand himself and to get more involved with the prison ministry. Penn and I would often go to the prison to visit, sometimes bringing my stepdaughters with us. Karen encouraged him. Sometimes she would come over for dinner. We would have a lot of fun but talked seriously, too. Penn got really involved in Karen's vision. It was wonderful for him, and it was wonderful for me.

In 1986, during our first year of marriage, Penn and I worked out of a bingo hall that we used as a clinic for refugees who were awaiting entry into Canada. These refugees were always in need of housing. I thought maybe we could have some refugees stay in our home, but my husband wasn't comfortable with that. So we compromised; we took in foster children. Penn had five daughters from two previous marriages, but he knew I felt I had a lot to give a child. When our first foster child came, Karen was my main support and was really encouraging. She was really, really essential for me at that time.

Penn and I supported Karen's life and work at the new HOPE House on Grider Street. She wanted to make it a home. She got exercise equipment for the guys and other things to keep them involved. She was always thinking about what do they need, what would help them in their transition, how do we keep them occupied, and how do we keep them eating healthy? She just loved these guys. It was an amazing thing. Her guys. She was the perfect mother. She was stern, she had her rules, and she had realistic expectations. She pushed them and chided them when they weren't doing well. And she stuck by the rules. If you broke the rules, Parole was notified. But Karen followed up on those who slipped.

~ *HOPE Hospitality House* ~

As HOPE House progressed, Karen initiated another ministry, HOPE Hospitality House, a place for out–of–town family members to stay while waiting to visit their loved ones in area prisons. I remember her saying, "Maybe we could set up a house where families could stay that would encourage them to visit the inmates."

The former convent of St. Matthew Church was available and had ten bedrooms. Like HOPE House, Karen was always thinking about how to make this more like a home. She asked her family and friends to each take one room and buy furniture, bedding, and decorations for that room. Each room was beautiful, homey, and very welcoming. Visiting families were welcome at a minimum cost, if they could pay it. Along with HOPE House and HOPE Hospitality House, Karen also ran a van service. The van took people from our area and guests from Hospitality House, as there are no buses from Buffalo to the area prisons.

Karen felt strongly that her guys needed to give back to the community. She developed a Teen Center at SS. Columba–Brigid Church and staffed it with her guys from Bissonette House. It was a safe place for teens to go on the weekend, and this gave the guys an opportunity to develop their own sense of responsibility, as well as do something positive to give back to the community.

Her Holiday Project provided Christmas and Easter packages to 2,300 prisoners. In the preparation, Karen would involve as many high school students and community and parish groups as possible. She worked with teachers to have elementary school children make cards for the inmates, which, she often said, were their favorites.

~ *Becky* ~

During this time, Penn and I were foster parents. In 1995, five–year–old Becky came to live with us. Becky was a delight and joy to us. She had spark and zest. My husband bonded with her completely. Penn and I really wanted to adopt Becky and, when she was seven, we were able to do so. We asked Karen to be Becky's godmother, and she stepped right in with support and encouragement, no pushing, just the exposure to her. She would come over and play with Becky and really enjoyed her. Karen would always let me know what a great job I was doing when at times I felt I was doing a pretty crummy job.

Becky, a friend of hers, Karen, and I used to go camping together. Karen loved the peace and fun of camping and would run with the kids and fall down on the ground with them. She was a kid herself. There was a part of Karen that had this innocence. She was childlike, but not childish. She didn't care what you thought.

During those years, when she had time to talk about a new idea, Karen would bicycle over to our house and share things that were going on with her. She sometimes told us about her dreams which were very powerful for her. She would know there was a message in them. Whatever the message was or whatever it foretold would happen. I used to feel goose bumps down my back because I don't have that mystical communication power and she clearly did. She knew it was a rare and special gift. Sometimes the message was about things she did not want to know and that would scare her.

I think Karen felt comfortable with me. I'm not a judgmental person. You could tell me anything and I'm not going to criticize you for it. I often saw the human side of Karen. She was a wonderful human being who had all the frailties of a human being, which made her even more precious and more special to me.

I could always count on Karen to celebrate my family's joys and share in our sorrows. This was especially true when Penn found out he had cancer and when he died in 2000. It was really hard on Becky and me. Karen went out of her way for us. She was just there. She had known Penn, and it was a personal grief on her part also. She knew what I was going through, and we could talk and share things. She was so understanding of Becky's and my needs. We could turn to her for anything. She was present in every way possible. Through it all, our friendship grew, as did her ministry.

~ *Karen and Hospital Ministry* ~

Erie County Medical Center (ECMC), right across from Bissonette House, has a prison lockdown unit. Occasionally, the hospital would get prisoners who were very sick or were dying. The families would come in from out of town, and they would either stay at Hospitality House or occasionally at Bissonette House. Karen became very involved in ministering to the sick and dying prisoners and their families–taking care of all the details that the families would face. In later years she would provide the same support to families with a loved one who was a victim of violence. A week before Karen died, she became a chaplain at ECMC and that would have given her even greater access to patients and families.

During the existence of HOPE Hospitality House, it was very difficult to find volunteers for all the services needed for this ministry. It became clear that the house was not sustainable. Karen had almost a mystical sense. She talked to God and God talked to her and she knew she had to let go of HOPE Hospitality House. She was heart broken. She was, however, very grateful when it was purchased for homeless veterans, a good mission. The sale was finalized just weeks before her murder. The van service that was connected to Hospitality House continues through a few volunteers, but more are always needed.

~ *NONVIOLENCE begins with ME!* ~

As the years passed, Karen began to develop more concern, not just about prisoners' and ex–offenders' needs, but about violence, the victims of violence, and forgiveness. It was an evolution of awareness. Karen was always evolving. She had all this energy, and she knew how to channel it. Once something got settled, she didn't sit back and watch; something else was mulling in her brain and it would come forth. She wasn't giving up on her guys, wasn't giving up on their families, but now she was concerned about the victims of violence and the impact on families. It was the next logical step. We must forgive and we must support.

I can remember Karen taking the pledge of nonviolence and her telling me that, if she were ever murdered, she would never want her murderer to be executed. It was morally repugnant to her. She believed even the worst "gangbanger" had some spark of humanity and a family that loved him. She was against all violence but specifically focused on interpersonal violence and street violence.

Becky at Bissonette House Peace Pole

In 2003, she began a nondenominational liturgy at Ephesus Cathedral (the former St. Bartholomew Church) called "Pledge to Nonviolence." Karen invited many people and the different groups they represented to make a one–year pledge of nonviolence. She especially wanted to include the kids, and I remember her asking Becky if she would carry a sign, "Girl Scouts of America." Becky's scout troop had made the Peace Pole that remains at Bissonette House.

During that winter Karen also began to minister to the victims of violence and their families. She held a Christmas party in 2003 for the children and siblings of homicide victims. She also organized gifts for the parents to give out in their homes on Christmas Day. The following summer she began another ministry, placing crosses representing each homicide victim in Buffalo in the Peace Park behind Bissonette House. There would be a cross for each person killed in the previous twelve months, and it would have the name of a homicide victim, age, and date of death. Loved ones would drop by to remember their son or daughter or husband or wife or friend who was honored with a cross; they appreciated the beauty and the quiet of the garden. In the summer of 2004 she changed the name of the "Pledge to Nonviolence" service to "Remembering and Pledging." Now we were not only pledging to nonviolence in our own lives, but we would also remember the victims of violence. The name of each victim was called out, and a candle was lit for each person. Speakers would challenge us

with ways to live nonviolently in our own lives.

Things were speeding up; Karen pushed to get more and more done. In 2005, at the Remembering and Pledging service, she distributed lawn signs that said: "NONVIOLENCE begins with ME!" She had 1000 ready, some written in Spanish. They began appearing around the city. But that wasn't enough; she had to do more.

~ Prayer Vigils at Homicide Sites ~

That same summer she began concentrating even more on the homicide victims and their families. She joined P.E.A.C.E. (Parents Encouraging Accountability and Closure for Everyone), a group of families who had lost loved ones to homicide. Karen introduced the idea of putting up a wooden dove with the victim's name, date of death, and age at the site where the murder occurred. She would come over to my house, and we would go down into the basement to cut out the wooden dove and paint it. Within a day or two of the homicide, the dove would be placed at the site during a prayer vigil. The dove indicated that this was sacred ground; someone lost his or her life here. With the visible symbol, people would remember, "Oh my God, someone was killed here." The dove would stay at the site. Sometimes a minister or priest would come to the prayer service for the victim, but Karen was always there. More and more doves went up. As it got colder outside, fewer people came, and many times Karen and I would be the only ones at the vigil. I remember that one of the victims was found in the Black Rock Canal; about four of us went over to the little island that was right near the spot where the body was found. It was summertime, so we brought some flowers. When Karen saw other people on the island, she went up to them and said, "This is what we are going to do ... ." She invited them and they joined us. We had this little service and put the dove up to commemorate this woman's life and tragic death. I often heard Karen say, "I don't care where they die; we're going to go and honor them."

~ Days of Peace Dove ~

Another thing Karen wanted to do was mark the days of peace, the number of days without a homicide in Buffalo. Again, she wanted the dove symbol, a big dove. How big could such a dove be? She got a machine that could put the dove image up on the wall and made a pattern that was the size of a piece of 4'x 8' plywood. Now we are down in my basement again, trying to see

SHARON CANTILLON/The Buffalo News

Karen next to her Days of Peace dove

how big a dove we could make, moving everything around so we could cut out this dove. Oh my God, this was Karen's dove. She was so excited. This was her baby. It was December 2005 when the dove went up. The dove was to serve as a public announcement for Buffalo to know how many days had passed since the last homicide. Karen would get up and read the paper to see if a homicide had occurred, and then, if there were a homicide, she would go out and change the number on the sign. By the time people would go to work at ECMC or drive down Grider Street, the correct number was displayed.

~ I Leave PEACEPRINTS ~

Photo – Patrick McPartland

Children at Bennett Park Montessori School gather to honor Sister Karen's life

As she was working on her Days of Peace dove, Karen was planning something else. "We've got to get to the kids so they are educated to causes of violence and can learn to live nonviolently." What she wanted to do was get one sign that she could give to young people who pledged to nonviolence. She decided on a smaller, cutout dove because kids would like that. She played with different words and phrases, but she finally chose "PEACEPRINTS." "As we go through life we leave fingerprints, why don't we leave peaceprints, little acts of kindness?" It was back down into the basement to design the peaceprints dove. Karen had the dove lawn signs printed, then arranged for the inmates at Attica Correctional Facility to cut them out. She hoped that they would be encouraged to say, "I Leave PEACEPRINTS," like a mantra, as they cut out each one. Sister Rosalind Rosolowski, a chaplain at Attica, drove back and forth between Bissonette House and the prison in what she called the "dovemobile" during February and March of 2006. High school volunteers at Bissonette House placed the metal stakes into the cutout doves.

Karen wasn't sure how or when she would unveil the peaceprints doves. She discussed many possibilities but had not settled on a plan. Nevertheless, there were 2,000 waiting and stored in the attic. It was at her funeral on April 14, 2006, when "I Leave PEACEPRINTS" was introduced. It was like she almost knew that there would be a very special event for the inauguration of the peaceprints doves, like she was leaving us her peaceprints.

When people came out of Karen's funeral and held up the "I Leave PEACEPRINTS" doves, I was off to one side, away from any media cameras. In *The Buffalo News* the next day, there was a photo of me right in the middle of a large group raising the peaceprint dove. Then I believed Karen was telling me to carry on her nonviolence ministry: the crosses, the doves for the homicide sites, the merchandise, and the advancement of the "I Leave PEACEPRINTS" and "NONVIOLENCE begins with ME!" signs. It's been a lot, but I have help now, though never enough.

Last year I took the garden crosses to my basement where I refinished and painted all of them. It was quiet, just me making the crosses as nice as I could so they would be ready to go for the next summer. As I carry out these projects, I feel close to Karen and am given the energy and strength to continue on her behalf.

From Sister Karen's Journal

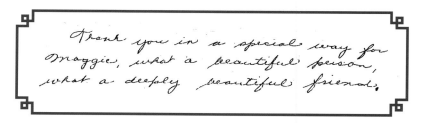

SHARON CANTILLON/The Buffalo New

"Maggie" amidst Peaceprints signs in Bissonette House basement

MARGARET "MAGGIE" McALOON, M.D., is a mother, physician, teacher, friend, and peacemaker. Maggie enjoys being with her daughter, tending a vibrant garden, and promoting peace and nonviolence with doves for prayer vigils and crosses for the Peace Park. Maggie also makes available peaceprint signs, shirts, jackets, pins, bumperstickers, and stationery at community events.

For information on "NONVIOLENCE begins with ME!" and "I Leave PEACEPRINTS" signs or other related items: www.hopeofbuffalo.org.

Sister Karen's Awards and Honors

Community Service and Recognition Awards

Homeless Alliance

West Point

Back to Basics

Weed and Seed

St. Martin de Porres Parish

New York State Division of Parole: Linda Mills Community Service

National Federation of Just Communities of Western New York

Sisters of Social Service

Masten Block Club

Durham Avenue Block Club

Delavan/Grider Block Club

Faith and Justice Awards

Gaudete Medal from St. Bonaventure University

"Faith Based Award" of the Community Action Organization of Erie County

President's "Where Eagles Fly" Award of Group Ministries, Inc.

Peacemaker Award from Jesus the Liberator Seminary of Religious Justice

St. John Eudes award from Christ the King Seminary

Peace and Justice Award from the Erie County Coalition Against Family Violence

Lifetime Achievement Award from the Capone–DeSimone Institute for Peace and Justice

Service to Mankind Award from the Sertoma Clubs of Buffalo and Allegany

Community Honors and Recognition

Induction into the Western New York Women's Hall of Fame

The Buffalo News Outstanding Citizen Award

Portion of Grider Street named "Sister Karen Klimczak Way"

(City of Buffalo)

Sister Karen Klimczak Memorial Award for a Victim Assistance Provider

(Victim Assistance Academy, State University College at Buffalo)

Peaceprint Award by Cephas Prison Ministries of Buffalo and Rochester

Window in SS. Columba–Brigid Church created in Sister Karen's memory

Conference Room dedicated to the memory of Sister Karen Klimczak

(New York State Division of Parole, Buffalo, New York)

DEREK GEE/*The Buffalo News*

Part II

Watercolor of Bissonette House by Roger Cook

Leaving Peaceprints on Our Hearts

Susan Klimczak

Sister Karen was thinking one day about how people leave a mark when they act in the world. She thought, "We leave fingerprints and footprints, so why can't each of us also leave peaceprints on the people in our lives and on the communities where we live?"

Anyone close to her experienced the everyday impact of her faithful efforts to imagine a city and a world where there is peace and justice. Every step Sister Karen took reflected her belief that we can build a "City of God," a city and world where each person can grow in grace and potential.

"Leaving peaceprints" starts with everyday efforts to believe another world is possible. We have daily opportunities to imagine and hope as Sister Karen did. Each of us can believe we can change. In groups where we gather together to worship, govern, serve, educate, and work, we have the ability to solve even the thorniest issues in our lives and communities. We can fearlessly search our hearts and find the courage to feel deeply that we are all connected. No one really lives and acts alone.

On April 22, 2006, Father Roy Herberger said in his homily, "I know Karen would have forgiven the man responsible for her death." Yes, Sister Karen would have forgiven Craig Lynch, because she tried to remain connected to her life's great teacher, Jesus. Sister Karen died on Good Friday, the very day when Jesus begged God to forgive those who put him to death: "For they know not what they do."

But Sister Karen would also have forgiven Lynch for another reason. She embraced him as her brother. She did not run from his suffering, but rather shared in it. She connected with what it was like to walk a mile in his shoes. She understood the wisdom of "There, but for the grace of God, go I." She knew that anyone can struggle with addiction.

To honor Sister Karen's life and memory, imagine a world blessed with justice and peace. Leave a peaceprint on the world every day. Forgive someone who has hurt you. Love the unlovable. Ask yourself, "How can I contribute love to this situation?" Be willing to consider that much of the suffering that people experience is not their fault. Don't turn away from suffering when you see it. Work for justice and peace.

Like Thomas from the Christian Gospel, put your fingers in the wounds of Jesus. See and feel the real impact of practices that make us separate and unequal, based on our income, our skin color, our family heritage, our nation of origin, our immigration status, our sexual orientation, our neighborhoods ... We are all connected and loved. Sister Karen lived it. We can, too.

An advanced doctoral student at the Harvard Graduate School of Education, **SUSAN KLIMCZAK'S** *life and career have been shaped by her relationship with her aunt, Sister Karen. Susan works in a program that brings together inner–city youth from different cultural backgrounds and neighborhoods to learn emerging technologies and sciences. (Learn 2 Teach, Teach 2 Learn Program)*

Witnesses to Peaceprints

Prison Ministry

I so much want to share in and with the poor, the prisoners, those who are so looked down upon by others. I offer you my tears of fear that this may not be possible — touch me — lift me up — make me one with those who are so much a part of me.

Lord, you are alive in so many of these men's lives. I now know it is possible to be catalyst of change in a person's life.

Finding Trust: Antwan Diggs

Judith Fitzgerald–Dolan

Mayor Byron Brown, Antwan Diggs, Sister Karen, and Oswaldo Mestre, Jr.

On a hot summer morning on Buffalo's East Side, I interviewed Antwan Diggs Sr., program coordinator for the Buffalo Weed and Seed Program Initiative which works to reduce crime and blight in specific city target areas. I met him at the "safe haven" of SS. Columba–Brigid Teen Center, cofounded by Sister Karen and Father Roy Herberger. When I arrived, Antwan was in a meeting with some good–looking teenage boys who politely let me in.

I commented to Antwan that he had to be doing something right to get these young guys up, out, and listening to his no–nonsense instructions. Antwan shook his head and said that if these guys learned only one thing, he hoped it would be: When they have a job, they should be there on time, ready to work.

This very teen center had been Antwan's "making" and could have just as easily been his "breaking" during the years he lived at HOPE House. He had been a teenager who grew up too fast in Philadelphia, burning all of his bridges including family ties. He left Philly for New York City and for the next ten years found himself mired down in a world of easy drugs, finally ending up in jail for three–and–a–half years. "After you do about six months in jail, once you start getting your mind back, you realize jail is a whole lot better than being a homeless bum on the street."

At Watertown Correctional Facility, Antwan earned his GED and started college. When he was released, he did well for eight months and then relapsed. Antwan explained, "There is a major transition that a lot of people don't realize. At Watertown, I had responsibilities such as teaching. I went right from that achievement to being a bum on the street–no job, no nothing. You walk into three or four interviews and they say, 'We can't hire you; you're a felon.' That beats you down."

After several relapses while on parole, Antwan ran away for two years, got caught, and was sent to Collins Correctional Facility. There, an inmate introduced him to the possibility of HOPE House and told him to call this lady, Sister Karen. Sister Karen stayed in contact with him, so they already had a rapport before they finally met. "I was really excited about coming to Buffalo and getting another chance, because I was certain, if I went back to New York City, I'd be a bum on the street. The only thing I knew about New York City was getting high. I got to HOPE House and a lady named Judy showed me around, gave me a key, and said she was leaving! A key. I just couldn't believe it!"

There are two stairways at HOPE House, one for the guys and one that led to Sister Karen's room. Exploring his new home, Antwan was captivated by some drawings on her stairway created by a prisoner. He went up to look at them. Something suddenly shot past his peripheral vision. "Sister! You must be Sister Karen!" "And you must be Antwan and that's the last time you use these steps!" Years later, they still joked about those stairs and would race each other to the top.

"The daily routine at HOPE House was really basic. Guys are guaranteed a thirty–day stay, at the end of which you need a job. Sister Karen would catch you in the middle of the day and find out how it was going. 'Where were you? Were you looking for a job?' Maybe she could call somebody, pull a few strings. 'Are you sure this is what you want to do? Maybe you should go back to school. Did you try this?' She didn't judge you; she just wanted to help. At the end of thirty days, she gave me a bus pass and more time. If you were really trying, she would work with you. One day, she drove me up to Union Road and pointed out a whole bunch of stores where I could apply. But I was working on my associate's degree, and I really wanted to get into human resources. I had applied for this job at the YWCA. Sister Karen, on the other hand, said, 'You need to be applying for ten jobs a day.'

"Finally, on the eighty–ninth day, the lady at the "Y" called and said I had the job! I raced upstairs to tell Sister Karen and she said, 'I know, the lady already told me.' She was busy and that was Sister Karen. But later, she pulled me aside and gave me a key and said to go to the third floor and pick out seven things. The room upstairs had all new stuff, brand–new shirts, brand–new pants, and brand–new ties, all brand–new stuff.

"She was just a natural. No matter what you told Sister Karen, it wasn't going to shock her. There was a spirit that flowed from her that let you know that this person was here to help. Her specialty was getting people to do things, but she wouldn't overtax you. She found out what you could do and she allowed you to do it.

"When Sister Karen found out that I liked working at the Teen Center, she gave me the keys to open on Friday nights. I never told her that I was afraid. I knew I didn't want to disappoint her. I almost gave the keys back a couple of times because I wasn't sure of myself. For somebody with a former crack habit, there was a lot of equipment to be responsible for, but God blessed me! I KNEW SHE TRUSTED ME! I had burned all my bridges of trust when I left Philadelphia, and even my own family couldn't trust me! It was nothing that I ever shared with her; it was just something she started to do.

"One time, Sister Karen said she wanted to come to help teach the kids how to use the computers at the Teen Center. I told her that we could handle it on our own. I knew that she'd go right into her teacher's mode, which didn't go over very well with the kids." Antwan tried to "head her off" to save the teens from feeling like they were in school, especially on the weekend! Sister Karen quickly learned that Antwan was right and let people at the center handle the teaching from then on. "Right before she died, Sister Karen did something that really amazed me. She decided I needed a credit card for the Teen Center! Wow!

"No matter what job I get, no matter what interview I go on, I will still have to be subject to that question, 'Are you a convicted felon?' Yes. One of the things that impressed me about Sister Karen and always made me feel good is, to her, we were not convicted felons. We were 'her guys,' bottom line. I want to show you a picture." The photo with this article is of Antwan when he was called for his first official duty to speak at a press conference as program coordinator for the Buffalo Weed and Seed Program. You see him standing in front of the microphone with Sister Karen standing right behind him, "willing" him on.

JUDITH FITZGERALD–DOLAN, *mother of two children, is a social activist for environmental issues, with particular concern about global warming.*

Meeting Christ in Prison

Lord, when did we visit you in prison? (Matthew 25:39)

Sister Rosalind Rosolowski, CSSF
*as told to **Eleanor (Dolacinski) Ash***

He was a towering figure, standing behind the infirmary plexiglas. Neither germs, nor healing words, nor touch could be exchanged. I recalled Father William McNamara's deep voice giving me his fundamental rule about ministry: "The most important thing you can do is be." So in that moment, all I could do ... the best I could do ... was put my hand up against the glass that separated us. Then the man put up his palm on the other side, directly opposite mine. We stood in silence, together.

On another day, a man who was keeplocked (restricted to his cell) was called to my office. I had to tell him the news that both his wife and his mother had died. The man wept. We sat in silence. No words could fill the moment.

In prison ministry, I am in touch with the rawness of life. Here many people have been directly affected by drug and alcohol dependency, by mental illness, by poverty. This contact influences the way I act and pray and live my religious vows.

My personal awareness of the vicious cycles of abuse and crime came during a course in juvenile delinquency at Canisius College. We had been discussing the cycle of prostitution. The teacher, a former probation officer, posed this question to the whole class: "How do we stop this? Who has the kind of clout or power or credibility that would make a difference?" I think my pen accidentally dropped off the desk. I bent down to pick it up and, before I knew it, heads were turned towards me because the instructor's answer was "the Church." I was the only religious there, still wearing the visible identity of the habit. A lot of students just looked at me, implying, "It is YOUR responsibility. YOU do something." And my response to them was "Oh, no, no! Now wait a minute. It's not just me."

The moment they said "Church," I knew what they were talking about, but at the same time my definition of church was not just those "in the cloth." However, from that night on I felt responsible. I prayed and asked for advice. I searched for different articles. Scripture was particularly important to me. What did Jesus do? How did he treat the prostitutes, delinquents, robbers? And there was always the great story of the good thief: "Today, (*Yes, today!*), you will be with me in paradise." (Luke 23:43) So perhaps before anyone else, a criminal was welcomed there.

In the 1980s, thinking about prison ministry was out–of–the–box for my religious community, because the order had what can be called a "corporate" ministry versus a "single" ministry. (In corporate ministry, a community serves one or two ministries as a group, such as teaching in a school or working in a hospital; in single ministry, a person responds individually to a particular need.) In serving God and others, both ministries are good, but they are different. I continued asking, questioning, searching. No matter where I went, in what city or town or at what conference, the answer was the same: If God wants you there, you will get there. If God wants you to do that kind of work, you will do that kind of work. Be patient and it will happen. I was not so patient, but the journey towards serving Christ Incarcerated was filled with valuable experiences.

I learned much from religious sisters and brothers and "Fathers" who were/are my colleagues and inspiration, but my natural father also showed me where to put the true focus: not on the crime, but on the criminal. One day my father was attacked by a switchblade–wielding nineteen–year–old who was on drugs. My father pressed charges, but when he saw his attacker in court, he requested that the young man get treatment rather than a prison sentence. In his decision, my father taught forgiveness. He hated the sin, but loved the sinner. Such is the call for every follower of Christ. The way is not easy.

As a prison chaplain, I ask myself, even when the human spirit is crushed: "How can I offer hope ... hope not only to the incarcerated, but to their family members, especially the children?" for they, too, are "imprisoned," emotionally, psychologically, financially, and socially. One program to help them is the appropriately named Hope Van Services, which transports local and out–of–town visitors to prisoners at Erie County Medical Center (ECMC), Attica, Wyoming, and Wende Correctional Facilities.

And what about the eighty-five percent of those incarcerated who return to society? What programs are in place that address the problems which exist for both the former prisoners and their families? For example, a family may have learned to finally live without the person, so how do they now reintegrate that individual into their lives?

At HOPE House, now Bissonette House, Sister Karen wanted to create a transitional center with a family atmosphere. Mentors guide newly released men. They pray together, assist in finding jobs, and help prepare for independent living.

Sister Karen and I had a deep sharing of our religious life and ministry. She had an excitement and a complete trust in God. When she was convinced that something was what God wanted, there was no stopping her. She followed a prophetic call, willing to speak the truth in the midst of confusion and injustice. I am reminded of the adage, "A prophet is not called to be successful, but to be faithful." Karen was faithful to the end. My father taught me forgiveness, and Karen was the mentor and friend who lived forgiveness. Forgiveness makes room for love. Perhaps only through forgiveness can we "be as mindful of prisoners as if [we] were sharing their imprisonment." (Hebrews 13:3)

Lord, when did we visit you in prison? And the Lord replied,
"I assure you, whatever you did for one of these least brothers of mine, you did for me."
(Matthew 25:39–40)

So although we think we are bringing Christ to those in prison, we actually are meeting Christ there. We are the ones who are being transformed.

SISTER ROSALIND ROSOLOWSKI, CSSF, *is a Felician Franciscan sister and chaplain at Attica Correctional Facility in New York State.*
ELEANOR (DOLACINSKI) ASH *is a long–time educator and volunteer in Western New York.*

Flowers from Sister Karen's garden

Photo – George Schaeffer

From Sister Karen's journal
July 17,1984

Couldn't help but think of the monarch butterfly. Yesterday when I saw it – it kept resting on the milkweed pod, as if getting its nourishment from it. Today it flew freely through the fields, no longer needing to get that nourishment from that plant. Yet, the milkweed plant will always remain a significant experience in the life of a monarch.

What are you trying to say to me Lord? Yes, I do want to "let go" and "let be." Help me never to "cling" and never to be afraid to fly freely – With you all things indeed are possible.

The Karen I Knew

Judy Hendee

Her guys described Karen as "real." They recognized her as a special person but saw her human side, too. She wasn't perfect. In her ministry helping them transition to society from prison, Karen's humanness was evident. The men always knew, though, that she did not play games. They knew Karen was authentic. She was human like them and the rest of us. She was "real."

For instance, Karen could be very impatient. She had so much energy both mentally and physically that at times it was difficult to keep up with her. When Karen had an idea about a project, she became single–minded in her determination to launch it. You either got on board or you might be temporarily banished from her line of vision. She could seem indifferent to those who weren't "on her page," but those of us who knew Karen well recognized that her "indifference" was more about her disciplined focus and not disinterest in us. Not everyone realized that.

Once a project was underway and going in the direction she wanted it to go, Karen would move on to another. That would become a chance for those left behind to be part of her new endeavor. However, sometimes we weren't exactly sure what Karen wanted: Most people did not automatically have her road map in their heads. She became used to people asking her to explain "the directions" on her maps. Once she understood what they didn't know, she was greatly enthusiastic in her explanations, and her enthusiasm was catching. Karen was an initiator, an organizer, and a visionary. She was also impatient to get a lot accomplished.

With the residents, she may have appeared to be impatient, too. Sometimes it seemed that she would lose interest in a resident whom she had been helping. But she didn't lose interest. She just knew when this man should start to take responsibility for himself. It was a function of her personality, but it was also a device to push a man up onto his own two feet. She was simply being responsible and "real." On the other hand, when someone sincerely needed help, Karen could be endlessly patient.

When necessary, Karen was clever enough to manipulate situations to get her projects done. I recall a morning after a particularly heavy snowfall. Karen asked the men in the house to shovel the driveway. They took their time getting ready, much to her frustration. So, out the door she went and began shoveling the driveway alone. Soon enough she was joined by the guilt–ridden residents who completed the job on her timetable–not theirs.

For those working in prison ministry, frustration is a given. When Karen welcomed a new resident, she knew that the *persona* of the man she met was only a small indication of who this person really was. The lives of these men are complicated. For instance, a resident might eventually overcome the huge monster of addiction, but often then needs to face possible issues about abuse, life skill challenges, homelessness, employment, or relationship problems. The constant frustration for Karen was that, over the weeks and months that a man lived at Bissonette

House, she gradually came to appreciate the depth and complexities of his needs. She also knew the painful reality of limited resources for ongoing personal rehabilitation. The only thing these men could count on was Karen's total caring and support. If they were trying, she was there for them in every way humanly possible. She kept up her relationships long after the men left the house. Even though hers was the kind of job where you knew you were successful if you didn't see a client again, she still wanted to know how things were going.

Karen admitted her shortcomings, even to the men at the house. She wanted them to know that she was working on becoming a better person, too. Her humanity made her approachable. It was a thin line to walk at times. Her personal growth was intimately tied to her relationship with "her guys." As she watched and shared in their struggles, she became more aware of her own limitations and was moved to find more meaningful ways to minister to the men. In serving them, she found new personal dimensions within herself. No wonder she said that if she had to choose between her ministry and being a religious, she would have to choose the ministry. It was her vehicle for personal and spiritual growth, and she knew it.

Karen's greatness lay not in some otherworldly saintliness that made her different from us. It lay in her humanity. Every day she lived with her own frustrations, disappointment, impatience, mistakes, and her daily struggle with control issues. Yet even with her human limitations, Karen was determined to love these men, accept them, give them a chance. If she were a saint, we could not identify with her, could not be inspired by her, and could not know that we, too, can live more fully and with more love. We "ordinary" humans need to remember that we can make a difference in peoples' lives, even as we struggle with our own frailties and mistakes as human beings. Karen is someone who showed us how.

*A semiretired counselor and teacher in county and state correctional facilities, **JUDY HENDEE** joined the board of HOPE in 1994, served six years as president, and continues to be an active board member for Bissonette House. Judy is an avid outdoorswoman who enjoys hiking, canoeing, and traveling, especially when the trips involve being with her children and their families.*

Cooking for Sister Karen's "Guys"

A Conversation with Sister Mary Anne Butler, SSJ

Sister Mary Anne Butler, SSJ

Dea McKenna McAuliffe

"Karen always called them 'the guys,'" said Sister Mary Anne Butler, who was drafted as chief cook and bottle washer at Bissonette House. "She grew up with nine brothers, so I think 'the guys' was a natural carryover. I loved hearing Sister Karen joke with them in her quick and witty style. One man, for example, was very slow about everything he did and Karen greeted him one day with, 'Hey, Speedy, how you doin?' I could see how he enjoyed the warm affection."

Sister Mary Anne saw Karen apply her love of God to the men in so many little ways. "She knew that God loves us just the way we are and that made it easy for me to love them, too. I could just relax and be myself, and through my cooking I could give them some of the love they needed."

One day, Sister Mary Anne whipped up her own brownie recipe, adding Hershey's syrup, extra chocolate chips, and lots of walnuts. A few of the men arrived home from work just as she took the experimental batch out of the oven.

"You better try one of these," she said when they came into the kitchen. "I don't know if they're any good." A few bites later, one of the men said, "Sorry, Sister, but these are terrible! I think you better give them to us and we'll get rid of 'em for you." Loud guffaws followed–along with another round of brownies!

Because of Karen's personality, Bissonette House was a place where the men found it easier to express their love, too. At one point, Sister Mary Anne was ill and absent from her kitchen for quite a long time. When she walked into the house on her first day back, one of the men was on the telephone. He hung up the phone and hurried to give her a big bear hug. "He showed so much love, and that's because of the atmosphere that Sister Karen created and nurtured every day," commented Sister Mary Anne.

So many ideas and recipes bounced around in Sister Karen's head, and at one point Sister Mary Anne looked longingly at ads for a rotisserie that would cook several meat items at once. When she was able to visit a niece who works for the city of Las Vegas, Sister Mary Anne made a request: "I'd like you to take me to one of those casinos." Her niece seemed surprised, but Sister Mary Anne shared that she had saved a bit of money and just wanted to win enough to buy a rotisserie for the guys. Nothing more.

Her eyes sparkled as she explained that when she dropped her last two quarters into the slot machine, she hit for 1500 quarters–enough to buy the "deluxe size" rotisserie she had seen advertised! Back in Buffalo with her fortune, she and Sister Karen estimated that they had enough money left for not one, but TWO parties for the guys.

One was a birthday party with all the trimmings, which left many of these street–smart men close to tears. Most had never had a birthday party before–and here were balloons and paper streamers and a luscious cake and singing voices! Sister Karen had lovingly arranged every detail.

"You know," Sister Mary Anne mused, "years ago, I left the teaching career I loved in order to become a nurse, which I also loved. After years as a nurse, I had to retire because of a back injury. Later, I enjoyed working in the SSJ archives. But when the opportunity to cook for Karen's guys came along, I realized that God had saved my best job for last."

Ready for a birthday celebration at Bissonette House

DEA McKENNA McAULIFFE followed Sister Karen's ministry through her friendship with Sandy Carrubba, a longtime board member of HOPE House, later called Bissonette House. Dea is an Associate of the Sisters of Social Service in Buffalo.

53

— My mom ... as I realize what she is going thru healthwise I'm scared; I love her so much & we have been sharing at such a deeper level lately; when I talk to her about life itself I get so excited — as she advises me to always look for the good in a person, not his/her faults — I smile 'cause I hear myself constantly saying that...

— As she tells me how wonderful it is that I am living with persons of other religions, like my Jewish friend, I stand in awe as I realize how I assumed that she wouldn't understand & that's why I didn't openly share that info with her — why do I think I know all the answers??...

Mother Love

Hadley Pawlak Horrigan

Late one evening, parole officer Anthony Amico went on his usual rounds, checking on released inmates, most often in the homes of their mothers and grandmothers. The women who took in the parolees loved their sons and grandsons through disappointment, pain, and heartbreak. The men let them down but would not be abandoned. Not by them.

They were women who, perhaps, believed the unconditional nature of their love would save these men. When the women found themselves no match for the drugs that won their beloveds' affections, this belief was tested but usually regained once forgiveness took root. Officer Amico's rounds were to ensure parolees were home, drug–free, and making progress on finding jobs and getting their lives together. At one home, he was met by a parolee's grandmother. When she saw Officer Amico at her door, she began to cry.

"He left this morning," she said through tears.

Officer Amico interrupted to offer comfort. "That's a good thing," he replied, assuming her grandson had finally gotten a job. "He's moving on. Beginning his life as a real man. This is what we want for him." But the grandmother cut off Officer Amico's pep talk.

"No. He left this morning with my microwave, stereo, and TV. He's using again. He robbed me again." Her grandson returned to jail and would later, after his release, be again visited by a parole officer at his grandmother's home because she would take him back.

> *The heart of a mother is a deep abyss at the bottom of which*
> *you will always find forgiveness.*
> — Honore de Balzac (nineteenth-century French playwright and novelist)

How is it that a mortal woman can love a man with such ostensible completeness? Forgive and care for an imperfect, hurtful human being, just as God cares for imperfect, hurtful collective humankind? Human beings strive to be Godlike in many ways each day–mighty, invincible, all–knowing, in control. But is it possible to achieve Godlike love here on earth? A Jewish proverb suggests that God could not be everywhere, so he created mothers. But if mothers were placed here to mirror God's love perfectly, Officer Amico would not have had reason to meet Sister Karen.

When Sister Karen started HOPE House in 1985, Officer Amico worried for her safety. Some of these men, after all, were turned away by their own mothers. But he respected her. She was fearless, he said, but no fool. And she loved God, and these men, deeply. HOPE House, later Bissonette House, was a home. "She treated those guys like they were her children and gave them a real chance."

Men who couldn't reconcile with the women who raised them were embraced by Sister Karen. In her, they were reunited with unconditional motherly love. Because of that, many called her "Mom." The nine parolees who lived with her at a given time started their day with a 7:00 a.m. prayer and breakfast. They had to be home for dinner each evening. Every man had a house chore, was required to maintain his own room, and was expected to do community service. They lived as family.

"At a lot of halfway houses, guys sleep on couches or on floors, but she gave everyone [his] own room with a ceiling fan," Officer Amico said. "She went out of her way for them. Vouched for them. Drove them around. Testified for them. Helped them find jobs. Things a mother would do."

Sister Karen's way worked. She helped hundreds of men get their lives on track. "She believed that the more trust, the more respect you showed, the better the result," Officer Amico said. "Having someone believe in them did it."

And though these men were auspiciously blessed to have fallen under her care, Sister Karen included her "guys" at the top of a list she once wrote about the ways God spoiled her. She considered these men one of His greatest gifts.

How could Sister Karen, a woman who met these men as strangers, see through an exterior formed by years of addiction, poor judgment, treachery, and shame to find the potential of a good man inside? Potential even their own mothers and grandmothers sometimes could no longer find? Or more confounding: Fifteen years before she met him, she already loved a man named Craig so much that she would forgive him for murdering her:

I forgive you for what you have done and I will always watch over you,
help you in whatever way I can ...
— Sister Karen, in a letter to her killer, written in 1991

Sister Karen loved these men through disappointment, pain, heartbreak. Craig, who let her and a whole community down, would not be abandoned–not by her. Sister Karen, it seems, did not–or could not–distinguish between a flawed man on earth and God. Each of these men was where she found God.

Whatsoever you do to the least of my people, that you do unto me.
"Whatsoever You Do" song by Willard F. Jabusch

She once described her work with ex–inmates as a way for her to see brokenness in the eyes and in the heart of an individual. "And when the brokenness is there," she said, "then you can see God. And God becomes real." In Craig, she saw God. And in both, she knew love.

*A former AP reporter and award–winning freelance journalist, **HADLEY PAWLAK HORRIGAN** is currently chief of staff of Upstate Empire State Development Corporation. Hadley volunteers as an instructor of Rite of Christian Initiation for Adults in Buffalo's Catholic Diocese and is on the board of Pinnacle Charter School.*

Flower from Sister Karen's garden

Photo – George Schaeffer

A Love Letter

Dearest Karen,

I have been mourning the loss of you. Like for so many guys, you were the Mom I never had.

Since the first day I arrived on your doorstep in October 1995, you immediately saw more in me than I ever could. One of the first things you told me was that God sent me to you. I arrived at a time when your "empire" was flourishing. My building skills were my contribution. You, of course, gave much more than any of us. The more stumbling blocks that got in the way of your purpose, the more determined you became.

Sister Karen and Michael

Karen, I know that you established certain boundaries that you said you would not cross; yet, when you knew that what we needed was more important than the boundary, you did not hesitate to cross it. In my situation, I remember a time when I got myself in trouble once again. You bailed me out, and I was angry because you did. I yelled at you for wasting your time on me. I'll never forget what you said, "Be quiet, tie your shoes, and get in the car. Michael, don't you know who I work for?" Because of your intervention, I ended up with community service and a more humble attitude.

You had such courage, Karen. You challenged so many of us with your heart. I see today what you tried to teach me and all the others. The only true guidance we need in life is from our hearts. God put good into all of us. So many times you reminded us that there is good in us, and we would be fine if we could just learn to connect our heads with our hearts.

Since your tragic death, I find myself searching for the reasons why I now feel so much closer to you. I ask myself questions. Could your death have been God's plan? Was it that He sacrificed you so that those of us you touched so deeply would truly recognize what you were trying to teach us?

I miss you.

Love,
Michael

Editor's note: Because of his struggles with addiction, Michael returned to prison. During the time he spent at HOPE with Karen, he experienced his most successful sobriety. A sideboard that he built in honor of Father Joe Bissonette highlights his carpentry and cabinet–making skills. It remains in the front vestibule of Bissonette House.

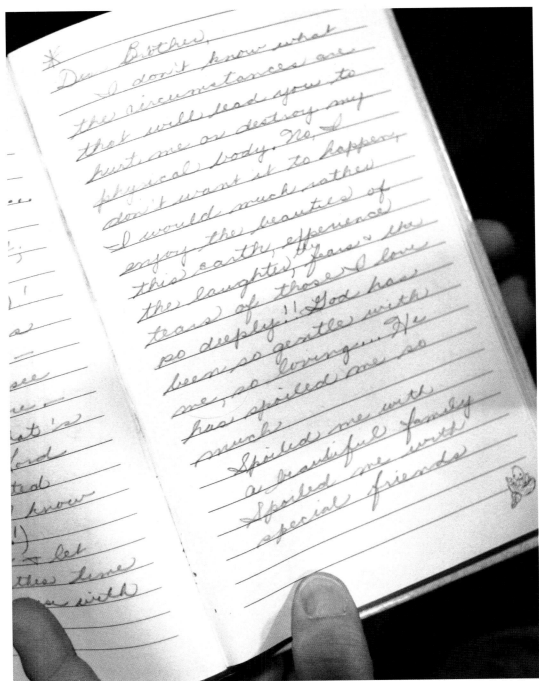

Dear Brother,
I don't know what the circumstances are that will lead you to hurt me or destroy my physical body. No, I don't want it to happen, I would much rather enjoy the beauties of this earth, experience the laughter, fears & the tears of those I love so deeply!! God has been so gentle with me, so loving... He has spoiled me so much.

Spoiled me with a beautiful family.
Spoiled me with special friends

"Dear Brother, I Forgive You ..."

Sister Jean Klimczak, OSF

**My sister, Karen Klimczak, SSJ, was murdered on Good Friday 2006.
Easter Monday 2006, Craig Lynch led police to her body.
He confessed to her murder.
At the indictment, Craig Lynch entered a plea of not guilty.
At his trial, Craig Lynch was found guilty of murder.**

At the time of Craig Lynch's indictment, I struggled with his plea. A plea meant there would be a trial and many more months before some closure. Those months became a time of anguish for my family and me, yet those months would prove to be providential: It was during that time that I found Karen's journals. Then I understood why I had to go through a time of uncertainty.

For me, forgiveness is understood most clearly through Karen's words. Karen's prescient, Christlike forgiveness characterizes her living forgiveness found in her journals and talks.

At Craig Lynch's sentencing, I read the prophetic journal entry written by Karen as Holy Week 1991 drew near. Words our community needed to hear. Words offering healing. Words of Karen's forgiveness and love.

Dear Brother,

I don't know what the circumstances are that will lead you to hurt me or to destroy my physical body. No, I don't want it to happen. I would much rather enjoy the beauties of this earth, experience the laughter, the fears and the tears of those I love so deeply!!

God has been so gentle with me, so loving. He has spoiled me so much.

Spoiled me with a beautiful family

Spoiled me with special friends

Spoiled me with a supportive religious community

Spoiled me especially with guys and those associated with Hope.

I am so grateful for all that life has touched me with

—the smiles and tears

—the gentle rains and the ferocious storms

—the sunshine and the dark clouds

I always loved the challenges of life because they brought me so much closer to the Lord who always held me in his arms.

Now my life is changed and you, my brother, were the instrument of that change. I forgive you for what you have done and I will always watch over you, help you in whatever way I can. The most difficult experiences in life can sometimes reap the greatest growth for us.

Continue living always mindful of His Presence, His Love and His Joy as sources of life itself. Then my life will have been worth being changed through you – – –

God bless

At HOPE House, Karen both fostered and lived a constant witness to what she considered essential qualities: unconditional, positive regard for others, and forgiveness. All of this flowed from the underpinnings of a deep prayer life. A journal entry states, *Prayer...the way of handling challenges...wow!* And there were many challenges.

Karen shares some of these challenges and examples of forgiveness in the following talk audiotaped at St. Mary of the Angels Church in Olean, New York, in 2002:

"A year–and–a–half before we moved into our building (HOPE House–renamed Bissonette House), the former St. Bartholomew rectory—a martyr met his death. Father Joe Bissonette was brutally murdered. The very room where he was murdered is a place where we, my nine guys and myself, pray together. We've got Christians, Muslims, Jews, Native Americans, all praying together.

"I had a dream once–where there was going to be a place where men and women, black, white, all different races, all different faiths were praying together. And all I could think of was, 'Hey, it can't happen in the Catholic Church. It certainly can't happen when I'm a Sister, because whoever heard of Sisters living with guys' Then all of a sudden, one day when we were in Father Joe's room, I looked around and that's exactly what it was: black, white, Native Americans, Christians, Jews, Muslims, religious, lay, all praying together. And in a place where a murder was committed!"

Karen teaches us through her stories:

~ *The Case of M&Ms* ~

"Talk about forgiveness! A guy named Joe was living with us. Things were going pretty well, when all of a sudden something happened in the house. This happens once in a while. Someone took something. When you take something from the house, there's something you should never take because I'll notice it immediately. You know what that is? Chocolate!

"There was a case of M&Ms. A big case of them, and they were gone. 'Where are the M&Ms? Someone took them.' All of a sudden I realized where they could be. I went to the corner store, and there my M&Ms were being sold at the store. And I said, 'Oh, okay!' So I found out who was responsible, but I wasn't going to tell anyone. So I said to the guys as we were gathered for prayer, 'I'd like the person who is responsible to acknowledge it.'

"Now that's a hard one, when you are talking about acknowledging something that you've done wrong and in front of a whole group. And so Joe said, 'I'm the person who took the M&M's and I just want to apologize for violating all of you and for violating this house when everyone's been doing so much for me.' So that was okay and then he said, 'Karen, can I see you after the prayer?' I said, 'Sure!'

"I'll never forget. We sat down in Joe Bissonette's room, in the prayer room. This is what my Muslim brother said to me. 'Karen, what I want you to do is, I want you to pray for me and with me. I want you to ask your God to forgive me.' As I prayed, there were tears coming down my cheeks and tears were coming down his, and what those tears meant was true forgiveness.

"I am still in contact with Joe and, when he left our house later, I gave him as much as I could in terms of food, because there is one way we respond to someone who does something wrong. That is, if they take from me, I give to them."

~ The Case of the Watch ~

"One of the guys had taken a watch that Father Roy Herberger, our board president, had given to me for one of the guys [someone else]. I put it down, and he took that watch. He admitted it and gave it back to me. So I asked Father Roy, 'What do you want me to do with the watch?' His answer, 'Give it back to him–give it to the person who took it. And perhaps, each time he looks at it, he will remember that it is important to acknowledge, to forgive, and to be forgiven.'

"So that young man was given the very item that he stole. When Father Roy did that, I was very touched by it.

"Sometimes when we respond to God in a sense of forgiveness, God likes to help us along. I've learned what it means to be gifted by God. When something goes wrong at the house, what do we do? We look for the good inside of something. That's our way of forgiving."

~ Celebrating Forgiveness ~

"Sometimes I've had things taken from me. And everybody knows there is one person who is responsible ... What do I do? I go to Dairy Queen, and I buy Buster Bars for everybody. I bring them home. The guys look at me and they say, 'You must be crazy. You know, Karen, you just had your bicycle stolen!' 'I know, but everybody is not responsible. And whoever it is, I appreciate the support I get, so let's celebrate each other. Celebrate life by eating these Buster Bars! Hey, I'll enjoy it. It's my favorite anyway.' So that's the way of celebrating. When things go wrong, we don't look at the wrong part of it. We try real hard to look at the right part of it."

~ *Prison and Priestly Vocation* ~

"Forgiveness! There was a young man named Roy Booker. He was a black man, 23 and married. He found his wife in bed with another guy. He went, took his bow 'n arrow and he killed the wife with it. He was put in prison in West Virginia. He had been drinking. He immediately gave himself up when he realized what he did. He was incarcerated with a life sentence.

"Then Roy Booker said he started to realize that he could reach out to the people who were in prison and help them out. He decided he wanted to become a priest. So he said to the Episcopal Church, 'I want to become a priest.' The Episcopal Church said, 'That's nice!'

"'Oh, come on. I really want to become a priest.'

"They replied, 'Why don't you just wait? Keep working and then you could become a priest. But you can't do it inside prison.'

"They knew he was in for life, but guess what? The governor pardoned him. Roy Booker got out of jail. He had been in for twelve years. He was doing so well that they decided to pardon him and allow him to be free.

"So Roy Booker went to the Episcopal Diocese and said, 'I want to become a priest.' The diocese said, 'Why don't you go and work for awhile?' So he went to work at IBM for a number of years. Then he went back to the diocese. 'I want to become a priest.' The Episcopal Diocese said, 'You really want to become a priest.'

"Well, Ron Booker is now Rev. Ron Booker. He is a priest in the State of Virginia in the Episcopal Diocese. He works with the poor. He goes to the prisons. He wants to give back to society, to make restitution. He can't bring his late wife back. He can reach out to others."

~ *Tears of Remorse* ~

"I have to tell you something about a young man. I'll call him Ed. Ed said to me one night, 'If I tell you why I was incarcerated, you'll hate me and you'll never want to be my friend.' He told me how he had been using drugs, and he was out of it–in the sense that you actually don't know what you are doing. He was out of it to such an extent that he hurt somebody. He started crying because he was so sorry about what he had done. When he saw that person in court, with a black eye and scars, he just lost it and said, 'I'll never, ever, ever, touch drugs again.' He hasn't. He was crying and he said, 'Once you know what I did, you'll probably never want me near you.' Just the opposite! When someone is so humble, enough to admit what he didn't have to, that what he did was wrong–how can I not say, 'It's okay.' He's making up for it twenty times over. Yet we judge."

~ *Reconciliation*~

"One of the guys said: 'You know, my mother said that she wouldn't take me back into her house, and you do. She said you've got to be crazy to do something like that.' And it's true.

"He couldn't go home, but he could come to us. Very often, we have them reconcile with the families. They go back to their wives, back to their children. So that's our main purpose. At HOPE House, it is 'Reconciliation, Restitution, and Giving Back.'"

After the talk, a person at St. Mary's said to Karen, "I would just like to thank you very much. I really needed to hear about forgiveness today, so thank you!" Karen's response was, "I just want to say we are always, always in need of forgiveness!"

In her own words and life, Karen witnessed the meaning of forgiveness. She did her part. We are called to live as sisters and brothers. We need to go to God and let God help us along. Karen challenged us to leave peaceprints of forgiveness, each of us in our own unique way. Now it is up to us.

Currently a chaplain in the Buffalo area, **JEAN KLIMCZAK, OSF**, *has served as a pastoral minister in hospitals and parishes in New Jersey and in the New York City area. Through her efforts, Sister Karen's spirit and vision continue to bless the people of Buffalo.*

HARRY SCULL JR/The Buffalo News

Karen, Little Sister of the People

Chuck Culhane

You'd have liked this today
another celebration!
Another bitter–sweet ending
beginning ...

Unlike the turn of your blessed life
the last mass, the end of St. Rita's
was planned, part of the many closings
a belated addendum to white flight
diocesan woes
and various erosions of the faith and flock–
but a celebration nonetheless.
Seats filled, scores of people stand along the walls
an organ blasts out its hopeful notes
a soloist belts out a gospel rhythm
and someone beats a bongo drum
while Brother Moe lights the last candle
its little light holding 153 years of memories.

I see you here little sister of the people
quiet, listening, watching, frizzy head bobbing,
foot tapping, wondering why there's no clapping
but, hey, there's hope,
and who knew hope better than you
hoisting it on the banner of forgiveness
raising the bloodied bones of Father Joe
stone by spirit–stone building an edifice of HOPE
for the wayward, the addicts, the very killers
forgiven before the act:
Father Joe's plea for them to do the better thing,
your letter of forgiveness a premonition of the risky odds,
God's will, it would appear, at awesome work.

Old friends, awash in memories
greet and hug each other.
Marge, smiling through tears
on the side–steps of the church
is telling everyone and pointing
to the purple pansy grown out of a crack in the stone
still alive and grown out of the stone step
still alive after snow and sleet and 20 degree nights
she points as though saying:
Can't you see this little miracle?

It was gone two hours later
maybe someone saw it as treasure
as remembrance, reminder.
"I took a picture of it," Marge said
to anyone listening.

Inside, slumped against the wall,
I knew you stopped by St.Rita's
on your Buffalo peace patrol.
I slipped my pen out of pocket
and began scribbling.
But how describe this race you've won?
that too many of us spend energy running from?

Back in my cell I taped up the picture Matt took of you
the afternoon of that endless Good Friday
the day suspended in the heart of the city
you, standing, with your sisters, looking down
I saw, just off the marble ledge
at the foot of your foot
the dove, the imprint
you at the edge of farewell
flower from stone,
our Sister.

11.26.07

Photos – George Schaeffer

Communities of Peaceprints

Organizations with Common Vision

We are asking individuals and groups to pledge nonviolence...I've always wanted to do something for victims...something against the violence in our city. And seeing so many wonderful people trying to work together, trying to do something to change it, that really makes a difference in my life. And I will do whatever thing I can do in my small way to create a more nonviolent society...we have to take the steps, whether this means standing up for what we think is right, whether it means being more nonviolent in interactions, we have to do our part. And as each of us does our part, the spirit will take over, of nonviolence.

Sister Karen (Field notes – 2005. Dr. Peter St. Jean)

From Sister Karen's journal

Help me to show
the importance of
talking things out;
of sharing with others.
Why? because by
sharing your pain;
your fears; your
anger - you show
another human being
that you trust that
person enough to
be honest with him;
knowing you won't
be rejected; you
will be loved
even more...

An Angel on Each Shoulder

Marc L. Fuller

When people ask me why I am driven 24/7 by my work as chairman of the Stop the Violence Coalition, I tell them I am doing God's work. Right here, right now. I live in the inner city of Buffalo, New York, a city that has the second–highest poverty rate in the country. When poverty's grip strangles the life out of people, chaos reigns. The men and women in the coalition want to restore order and bring justice to our streets. We want to offer hope and protection. We have to look at ourselves first. Nonviolence really does begin with me. My grandmother believed this and believed in me. She is always with me in this work.

My grandmother instilled God in me and always wanted me to do the right thing. A lot of what she taught did not hit me until I became almost grown. Like she always would say, "You don't need to fear death," and I, not knowing that all these years later I would be dealing with death first–hand, sometimes on a daily basis. The conversation never changed from the time I can remember right to the day before she died. As weak as she was, she talked to me for two straight hours on how to lead a good life. It was always the same conversation: Slow down, believe in God, and do the right thing.

One time when I was having legal problems, I "hid" on the streets for almost two years. I heard Grandma wasn't feeling well, so I decided to visit on her birthday. When I walked in, she looked at me and all she said was, "Where you been? You living two lives. You all here doing all this and keeping it from me. I know this isn't you." She didn't ask me anything else. I eventually came back around, got a chance to eat her cornbread again and a whole lot more. I did not ever want her to know what I had really been doing those two years. With the young men I mentor now, I find out if there are grandmothers in their lives. I ask them, "Is there anything you're doing that you wouldn't want your grandmother to know about?" If they say, "Yeah," I tell them, "That is the way to know that you shouldn't be doing it."

My grandmother told me I should be a preacher. I figure I am. In the coalition, we know the street, we speak the language of the street, and now we preach in the street. A lot of these young men have never been in a church. We bring the church to them. Even the worst thugged–out young man wants to know God still loves him, God forgives him, and he has another chance.

Grandma stayed on the corner of Wohlers and Riley for over thirty years, the first black family to move into that neighborhood. I remember when the drugs came into the area, my grandmother said, "This is my corner; they not going to run me off my corner. I fear no man, nobody but God." My grandmother was a one–person army. Her husband died just after I was born, so after Grandma raised her children, she spent a lot of years alone in that house. But nobody ever messed with Lillie B. Smith. That was her corner. Respect it. When people try to understand my energy, that's where it comes from, my grandmother.

Sister Karen had the same energy. The moment I met her I believed I had a connection with her that nobody saw but the two of us. I remember one night we had a prayer vigil, and it was dark and people were mourning. We was "in the hood" and Sister Karen was sticking out like a sore thumb. When I arrived, she said, "I'm so happy that you are here, Marc, because these vigils are not the same without you with us." She gave me the peace dove and she said, "At these vigils, this will be your part." I would offer her dove of peace to the grieving family and then hang it for all to know that, at this place, a loved one was slain. Sister Karen brought honor and respect to that place and to that person who is no longer here.

We had a very spiritual connection. It was something about her and I believe it was something about me. She was somebody who was sincere with what she was doing. It was no fraud; it was real. Always played the background, that was Sister Karen. I played the background, too, and that is how we connected. She told me we were going to move forward. "Marc, there are places that I can go that you can't go, and there are places you can go that I can't. That is going to make us a great team." She rubbed my hand because of the color of my skin. Sister Karen was honest. She was about helping those who couldn't help themselves. Just knowing Sister Karen became another part of this drive in me.

Before she died, Sister Karen was thinking a lot about the families of victims and the families of perpetrators. This had been on my mind, too. Even though a relative did this, we don't talk enough about that perpetrator's family–who didn't do anything. But now this family is labeled. A shame covers over the whole family.

Actually, my concern about the family of the perpetrator came to the forefront at Sister Karen's funeral, because I got a chance to meet the perpetrator's sister. She was just standing there outside St. Ann's Church, all alone. She told me she didn't feel she should be a part of it. I convinced her that she should go in; she finally took my seat reserved for the coalition.

What I witnessed with Sister Karen's family was they stuck to it for real. Because you can say things like forgiveness, but when it happens, do you really know if what you are saying is real? The Klimczaks even told the Lynch family that they would be welcome to go to Sister Karen's funeral. That's the real thing. That's like Sister Karen. Everything about forgiveness.

I know I have been tested about forgiveness, especially with two individuals who were murdered. I didn't know what I was going to do. You are promoting all this peace and then you get those calls. First, my friend of thirty years, Stacey Gust, was just visiting friends, and she was a victim of that quadruple homicide in 2005. Then in 2006, my oldest daughter was screaming on the phone: her fifteen–year–old brother Ke'one Littlejohn was killed. Now, I'm being tested. I'm out here telling folks how you can't retaliate, can't do this and that, and I'm being tested for real because this was a good and long–time friend and it was my daughter's fifteen–year–old brother. I knew what went through my mind. "I 'bout to get on the block! This is my people. This is how you got to handle this." Then I hear Lillie B. Smith, "You don't ever have to do nothing because God will always take care of anything that comes up against you." And I have to really, really believe that because I have a side of me that is just waiting to come out at any time.

It's like a recovering addict, a recovering alcoholic. They are always recovering. Most of us from the streets are always recovering, too. A slip from recovery is "just right there." You have these evil spirits around you, constantly knocking at your door to get out again, to ruin all the good we are doing. It would take only one episode to ruin everything. I fight that every day.

I see Sister Karen's doves on the telephone poles and trees all around the streets where people have been murdered, and I remember her power and commitment to people. I hear my grandmother telling me how to live and I feel her love. Her voice is always right here within me. When people try to understand how I deal with all the chaos of drugs and gangs and killing and people being crazy, I know why I carry on. I have an angel on each shoulder.

MARC L. FULLER *is chairman of the Stop the Violence Coalition, Inc., a group of volunteer peacekeepers who are determined to put an end to violence and bring justice to our streets through gang mediation, mentoring, GED programs, and keeping the peace at innumerable events in the city of Buffalo.*

Stop the Violence Coalition (STVC): PO Box 626, Buffalo, New York, 14201.
(716) 882–7882; stvcoalition@yahoo.com; www.stoptheviolencecoalition.com

"Buffalo Rising"

Photo – George Schaeffer

Teach me, Lord of Life,
how to eat my food with
awareness;
show me how to walk deliberately
rather than constantly run,
how to truly visit & be present
rather than merely exchanging
words.

Help me, Divine Friend,
to take my time in praying
to you.

Show me that it is good
just to "waste" time with
You in such acts as
enjoying a sunset or a friendship

With your presence & assistance
I will attempt to do all things
with mindfulness; slowly,
carefully & fully aware of what
I am doing.

Then, with your grace, I
shall find You, my God,
in those unhurried &
mindful moments.
A-M-E-N

We Have a Choice:

The Alternatives to Violence Project

Audrey Mang, SSJ Associate

"I've become a better communicator in my family." "I've received more affirmation in three days than in my whole life." "AVP allowed me to see inside of people and realize that we are not as different as I thought." "If I listen better, I will understand better." "I learned new and different methods for defusing conflicts." "I have learned to be more patient." "What I learned in AVP works in the real world."

We live in a world filled with violence. No one should have to live this way–hurting others and being hurt by the violence done to us. We in the Alternatives to Violence Project (AVP) think this can change and the place to start that change is within each of us. This is what Sister Karen was saying with her "NONVIOLENCE begins with ME!" signs. An essential belief of AVP is that there is good in everyone. We also believe that within the universe is a power that is able to transform hostility and destructiveness into cooperation and community, that this power is everywhere, and that we can tune into it.

The Alternatives to Violence Project began as a voluntary program for inmates in a New York State correctional facility. It spread outside the walls to community groups and is now offered throughout the United States and in more than forty-five other countries, many of them torn by war and other devastation. But violence causes harm in many ways, not only in the dramatic ways that hit headlines. We can so easily do violence to others when we insult or speak harshly, lose our temper, turn away, fail to respect the religion, race, or gender of others, gossip or push our own agenda without listening. If we are truly committed to nonviolence and want a peaceful world, these are the kinds of provoking behaviors that must change.

The Niagara Frontier Council of AVP has been working in the Western New York area for twenty years. In 2007 we moved to the SSJ Sister Karen Klimczak Center for Nonviolence where we continue to offer weekend workshops in which participants explore the causes of violence and investigate ways to resolve conflict nonviolently. AVP provides a safe environment of mutual respect with a series of exercises and discussions. It is experiential learning with a minimum of lecture.

No matter the makeup of those who come–inmates, teenagers, women religious, teachers, community folks–the fruits of an AVP workshop are the same: a stronger belief in themselves and their ability to deal with conflict and violence; practice in vital conflict resolution skills;

understanding the importance of empathizing with others (i.e., "walking in their shoes"); and, not least, experiencing the great unifying value of laughing together.

What is the connection between Sister Karen and the Alternatives to Violence Project? She had an unshakable belief that our responsibility as followers of Jesus is to look for and nurture the good in everyone. Sister Karen knew that our attitude and demeanor, our words and actions in time of conflict can turn a situation around. These are the basic principles of AVP. Two years before she died, Sister Karen took an AVP workshop and, because of the potential she saw for helping "her guys," began a conversation with the New York State Division of Parole to offer AVP as one of the program options for parolees. At the time of her death this had not yet been approved.

Will we always be able to prevent violence? Perhaps not every time, but each time that we respond nonviolently, we decrease the hurt in our world and increase the reconciliation and healing.

AUDREY MANG, SSJ Associate, served on the staff of the Center for Justice and the Western New York Peace Center from 1976 to 2001 and helped begin the SSJ Sister Karen Klimczak Center for Nonviolence in 2006. Since 1988 she has facilitated AVP workshops in New York State correctional facilities, in schools, and in the community.

Readers are invited to participate in an Alternatives to Violence Project workshop. For upcoming dates, contact the SSJ Sister Karen Klimczak Center for Nonviolence at 80 Durham Avenue, Buffalo, NY 14215, (716)362–9688, info@sisterkarencenter.org.
See also: www.avpusa.org and www.avpinternational.org.

Photo – George Schaeffer

Peaceprints sign on lawn in Buffalo

4530
6
×7
42

PIZZA
cheese

12:35

- my fear of letting go
- Jesus accepted
     people where they are at...
     he went out and after
     the stray sheep...
     His challenge
     ... to reach out &
     embrace the abortionist,
     pray for them
     ... to love the murderer
     and the victim
     ... to embrace those
     who "turn us off"
     ... to discover the
     wheat among the chaff —
     don't discard it —
     there may be a seed
     of wheat hidden
     within.
     ... to embrace all —

From Sister Karen's journal

Back to Basics with Elder James Giles

"'Sister K' took a battle that was not hers, personalized it, and became a force in the battle."

Evelyn McLean Brady

When you are in the presence of Elder James Giles, director of Back to Basics Outreach Ministry, you feel the sheer weight of the man's spirituality. That is why so many hurting people find their way to 906 Broadway where Elder Giles ministers to the homeless, the addicted and those transitioning from prison.

I was curious why Elder Giles, who is gifted in communication and administration skills, chose to work with people whom some consider outcasts and, sometimes, unredeemable. Elder Giles responds in a quiet voice, "At one time, I, too, was considered an outcast. But God said, "Not so. It is in our brokenness that we begin to see the evidence of God moving." James Giles's story is

Elder James Giles in background. In foreground: Lenny Lane {FATHERS}, and Jeffrey Crawford at Summit on Youth and Gang Violence, in Albany, NY.
~ November 15, 2005 ~

a story of brokenness and redemption, of "the evidence of God moving." It is the story of anyone who opens his or her heart to the power of God's grace and mercy.

During his college years, Giles let himself be pulled into the world of drugs–using and selling. This world eventually led him to further crime and the revolving door of prison. Even with the support of a caring family, a devoted wife whom Giles refers to as "my best friend," loving children and uncles who were strong, positive role models, for almost twenty–five years, Giles fell and rose in a cycle of crime. Heroin controlled James Giles. Then, in 1994 at Cape Vincent Correctional Facility when Giles was forty–three years old, something miraculous happened.

Giles describes the setting. "At Cape Vincent, the cells–our cages–are built four tiers high; each tier has a row of cells forty–eight across; opposite these cells are tiers of cells in the same configuration. There are 348 cells in that one area." Most of the men in that concentrated space were in their late teens and early twenties, ages when people often try to drown out interior feelings and thoughts with loud, external noise.

The level of constant clamor and endless commotion from the cells overwhelmed James. Yet, in the midst of the banging and the loud yelling back and forth, James Giles, alone in his cell, felt himself drawn into a circle of complete silence and stillness. James started to pray. He begged God for mercy and forgiveness. "I asked God for forgiveness, careful not to complain about my circumstance." As his prayer continued, a profound quiet enveloped Giles. His entire being was filled with unshakeable peace. He did not know how long the silence lasted, but he did know he was a changed man. He quotes scripture to explain: "The Spirit of God anointed me to preach the Gospel to the poor, to set the captives free, to mend the broken hearted ... ." After experiencing that circle of prayer, Giles knew he would never use drugs again. He realized that he had become one of God's disciples, and he would bring to others the love God had shown him. "Those of us who have come into His presence begin to develop the compassion that God has exhibited toward us," Giles shares, almost in a whisper.

When he was released from Cape Vincent, Giles left prison for the last time. Not long after, in partnership with another former inmate, Anthony Brown, with whom Giles felt a deep spiritual kinship, Back to Basics Outreach Ministry was founded. In his new ministry, Elder Giles would often run into Sister Karen, especially at prayer vigils for the victims of homicide. He called her "Mother Teresa on speed." Giles noticed that sometimes "Sister K" (his own name for her) would "jump out and do a prayer vigil and encounter the 'element,' and there would be strange components within this element that she didn't quite understand." She always wrestled with the fact that she was in "someone else's neighborhood," but Giles would tell her, "Just meet the needs. You're doing this not seeking your own glory, so don't worry if it is going to be accepted."

Giles knew that Sister K wanted the prayer vigils to reveal God's presence and to bring comfort to the families. At one vigil, Giles made a suggestion to Sister K: "I'd like to anoint this place so that what took place here never happens again." He continues, "I had my oil and I anointed the tree where the memorial was set up and we prayed for the family. Sister K was so appreciative that, from then on, she would call me, 'Are you coming to anoint at the next vigil?'" Giles explains that Sister K wanted to designate these places where life was taken to be places where new life could begin. With the doves, candles, and prayers, these killing places became symbols of sacred city soil.

Giles also recalls Sister K at meetings for various activities to promote nonviolence. "Whenever we wanted to publicize events, Sister K would come up with banners and slogans and signs and announcements. I used to tell her, 'One of you would set 1,000 demons to flight, two of you, 10,000 to flight, but three of you would set every demon in the world to flight. We would have no more pain, no more suffering.' "

Elder Giles adds with great seriousness, "Sister K took a battle that was not hers, personalized it, and became a force in the battle. You could always see the love that motivated her. She carried it around with her." That is the same love one sees in Elder James Giles.

Back to Basics Outreach Ministry can be reached at (716) 854–1086.

From Sister Karen's journals
1985

June 15, 1985

Lord... I feel so inadequate... why me?...
can I really be a part of a home
for ex-offenders?...

... for all fathers who are separated
from their families because of
imprisonment / that they may
turn toward you God as their
Father as a source of their strength

... that we may enable the
words that we listen to and
read become real in our lives

F.A.T.H.E.R.S.: Planters of Peaceprints

Tom O'Malley

Darkness cannot drive out darkness, only light can do that.
Hate cannot drive out hate; only love can do that.
— Martin Luther King, Jr.

Just a few blocks away from Bissonette House, Leonard Lane stands in front of his neat home on Buffalo's East Side. "I've lived here all of my life," he said. "This house was my father's and after he passed away I moved my family right in." Leonard, a twenty–year veteran of the Buffalo Fire Department, remembers Sister Karen quite well. "She was a warrior for peace. She was the General, and I am one of her foot soldiers."

As we talk, neighbors pass and wave. Lane's face lights up as he speaks with pride about this neighborhood and his place in this community. In 2001, not far from where we stand, a stray bullet from a street shooting flew into School 61. Even though no one was hurt, that bullet became the fuel that ignited Leonard and a group of men to band together to make sure that their children could have a safe and peaceful environment in which to learn. Thus, F.A.T.H.E.R.S. was born: Fathers Armed Together to Help, Educate, Restore, and Save. And restore they are, one child at a time. Leonard's face is open and sincere, a peaceprint stamped in a turbulent city. When he speaks of Sister Karen, he beams: "This feisty little woman came into our neighborhood. She was small in stature but mighty in her impact. She set the bar very high and inspired us to keep it there."

Today, F.A.T.H.E.R.S. keeps the bar high through action. Members spend their time in schools, speaking with children and providing positive role models for kids. Last year, F.A.T.H.E.R.S. rebuilt the playground at School 61. In the summer, they sponsored the "Dog Days of Summer," weekly cookouts for neighborhood kids. Leonard dreams of restoring the positive image of the father as a flesh and blood symbol for protection and stability in his community. He is planting seeds of his own.

Sister Karen's peaceprints are much more than cardboard signs. They are really imprints on the souls of men like the F.A.T.H.E.R.S. who have the faith and courage to push back the darkness. They are a powerful symbol of what can happen when a person puts his or her faith into action to drive out hate and let in light.

TOM O'MALLEY *has published essays and stories in The Christian Science Monitor, The Buffalo News, and numerous journals. He teaches at St. Francis High School and Canisius College in Buffalo, New York.*

Thinking About Sister Karen

Karima Amin

I first met Sister Karen Klimczak in 2004 while seeking information about Bissonette House. She was on her knees working in the "Peace Garden" behind the house. I thought she was the most curt person I had ever met. She barely glanced up at me and she answered my questions in a gruff manner that conveyed no warmth. In spite of what I thought was a negative first impression, her answers were comprehensive, and I realized later that she had shared more information than I had asked for. In fact, she gave me some priceless information that I could later use in advocating for an incarcerated friend and that I would use two years later in formulating the idea for "Prisoners Are People Too!"

When I saw her again, about six months later, I was surprised to learn that she remembered me, my name, and our prior conversation. She even remembered that I lived around the corner from Bissonette House. She asked about my incarcerated friend, who had just faced the parole board for the second time, and she asked how my work was coming along. She was genuinely interested in my desire to help a prisoner, and she really cared about how I was managing to take care of myself in the midst of my work. I had seen the two sides of Sister Karen Klimczak: "the iron fist in the velvet glove." Sister Karen was a tough, little woman–feisty and compassionate, strong and demanding. But fair.

I didn't know Sister Karen as well as some people, but I was proud to work with her as a member of the Western New York Reentry Coalition. She and I had many conversations over a three–year period. Most were brief, but I always learned something new about her and about myself. Sister Karen loved and respected all life. She didn't believe that any one person's life was more important than the life of another. She believed in second chances and in the possibility of redemption.

Sister Karen's death put a spotlight on some attitudes prevalent in this community: that all parolees are "scumbags" and "degenerates"; that all prisoners are "demons" and "animals" who should be locked up; that all halfway houses should be closed; and that Bissonette House is in a bad neighborhood. If Sister Karen were alive, I know that she would address each of these charges by providing empirical evidence, from her life and work, to prove them wrong. She would probably say that the criminal justice system needs to be dismantled and overhauled to honor the principles of rehabilitation, reformation, and restorative justice.

She lived with men who were formerly incarcerated, who had been punished, who had served time, whether that time was warranted or not. She also knew that parole was not a reward for good behavior. She viewed it as a vehicle for moving forward with one's desire to start over, to build anew, and to replace destructive behavior with productivity.

Sister Karen's death put a spotlight on the fact that we are all in this community together, even those who are imprisoned. Their families are here and these formerly incarcerated men, women, and children are coming back. Sister Karen would urge us to love, not hate; to help, not hurt; and to welcome, not ostracize.

KARIMA AMIN is a retired public school educator, performing artist (storyteller and drummer), author and community activist. She is the founder and director of PRISONERS ARE PEOPLE TOO! which seeks to enhance the community's knowledge of prison issues and criminal justice issues.

www.aclearwebcreation.com
www.wings.buffalo.edu/uncrownedqueens/Q/files/amin.htm

Lord, life can be so rough for others, help me to be a gentle, breeze in their lives. by listening to them by responding to them with a sense of care & love.

Lord, give me the courage to live in the light the challenging aspects of life, speaking out when being silent would be the safer, un Christ like response; to listen with great intent & openness.

when speaking would be a cover up & a stumbling block in allowing You to teach me how to live...

P.E.A.C.E. in the City

A Conversation with Teresa Evans

Lisa Murray–Roselli

Hope is a powerful, humming force that drives us through the night and into the next day. It is the reason why we go out into the world and work, go to religious services, maintain friendships, keep our families close, and have children. We are hopeful that life is worth our efforts, that life will be better in the future for our efforts. Though evidence abounds–on the news, in the stories of our personal lives, and in the general swagger of carelessness that seems to taint our culture–of a world that should be drained of hope, it flows still. Nowhere in Buffalo, New York, is that more apparent than in an organization called "P.E.A.C.E." (Parents Encouraging Accountability and Closure for Everyone).

In 1996, Teresa Evans, whose son was the victim of a homicide, joined forces with Leslie Jordan of Women and Children's Hospital of Buffalo Bereavement Services. They formed a support group called "Rebuilding Life after a Violent Death." Families began coming to this support group and sharing their stories. As time passed, it became apparent that more was needed to help these families. In 2003, members of the support group, with the cooperation of the district attorney's office, formed P.E.A.C.E. as a complementary support group to help families deal with the legal and business aspects of how to cope after a homicide.

The mission of P.E.A.C.E. is to provide support and assistance to families and friends who have lost a loved one to homicide. P.E.A.C.E. seeks to engage the authorities as they proceed through the stages of the investigation, arrest, and prosecution of the person(s) who are responsible for the murder(s).

For Teresa Evans, current president of P.E.A.C.E., and many other members, their commitment to the organization can be emotionally draining. She says, "[In addition to] the love of a close–knit family here in Buffalo, the support group is like a family [for me]; you can always go to another mother just to talk." Teresa Evans takes Christ's message of service very literally. Although she could have shut herself away after losing her son to violence, a tragedy that stays in her heart, she reached out for help and then took a leadership role in providing help for others who were suffering.

In June of 2005, Teresa met Sister Karen Klimczak. Together, they developed the idea of holding prayer vigils at the sites where homicides occurred. The vigils are moving for all who attend. The uncle of a murdered boy said, "After experiencing this prayer service, my heart has truly been changed. I am no longer angry and filled with vengeance. My heart is sorrowful, but I am at peace." Attendance at P.E.A.C.E. meetings increased after the vigils began.

Sister Karen quickly became the greatest ally of the P.E.A.C.E. organization. She loved the community in which she lived and worked, and families came to love and depend on her. The members of P.E.A.C.E. were very protective of Sister Karen and offered to accompany her as she ministered throughout the neighborhood, but Sister Karen brushed aside their concerns, feeling quite comfortable among the people she considered her own. Teresa remembers that, during one telephone conversation, Sister Karen said, "Teresa, I just love being with families. I just love being with the mothers."

Sister Karen's murder in April of 2006 was a tremendous blow to the community and to the members of P.E.A.C.E. in particular. They lost a good friend, a confidante, and an irreplaceable inspiration. But hope continues to motivate Teresa and all the members of P.E.A.C.E. When asked how she would like to see the organization develop in the future, Teresa responds, "I'd like to stop doing prayer vigils, and I'd like to see the people start healing. We have so many children left behind. I would like to see them taken care of, so they don't grow up to be angry kids. I hope that one day we will get the service providers who deal with grieving children. There are a lot of lost people, hurting people."

Until her vision of a city without homicide is realized, Teresa Evans and the dedicated members of P.E.A.C.E. will continue to do what they can to provide healing and direction for those families who lose a loved one to violence, especially the children. Sister Karen's spirit and example will continue to guide them, and her peace dove, seen on the ubiquitous signs throughout the city, reminds us all that: "NONVIOLENCE begins with ME!"

©2005 Peter K.B. St. Jean

Sister Karen joins P.E.A.C.E. members and others at prayer vigil.

LISA MURRAY–ROSELLI, a freelance writer and editor, is the mother of two little girls. Lisa and her husband, Paris Roselli, are members of the Sisters of Social Service Advisory Board. Those interested in contacting P.E.A.C.E. may call (716) 400–9762.

Fridays with Sister Karen

Matthew R. Smith

Photo by Carol Smith
Sister Karen at Stations of the Cross, Good Friday 2005

I knew Sister Karen for about ten years through the Buffalo Catholic Worker, a faith group that gathers on the first Friday of each month for prayer, study, and action. We meet on Fridays because that was the day Christ was crucified, and we desire to help the crucified people of our world. Over the years we have met at soup kitchens, halfway houses, peace centers, homeless shelters, and inner city parishes to learn about the needs of the poor and marginalized in our community and to discover ways to serve our neighbors in need. In a way our monthly meetings are like a slow—motion Stations of the Cross, a living "Via Della Rosa."

We liked to meet at Bissonette House because, like Sister Karen, we were attracted to the story of Father Joe Bissonette, a person of deep faith with a passion for peace and social justice. Father Joe was murdered, many say martyred, after opening his door to two young men in a spirit of charity and hospitality.

On the Fridays we met with Sister Karen, a Station of the Cross so to speak, she taught us lessons for our life of faith. We also learned about and participated in running Sister Karen's HOPE Hospitality House, a ministry that provided overnight hospitality and transportation for family members coming from out of town to visit their loved ones in area prisons.

At the last Friday meeting before her death, Sister Karen brought in a mother whose son was killed in a shooting in Buffalo. This meeting made real another Station of the Cross for me. As the African–American woman spoke of the loss of her son, I could begin to sense the grief Mary must have felt when her son was killed. After that meeting, I invited Sister Karen to join us for our second annual Good Friday Stations of the Cross walk in downtown Buffalo. I asked if she would bring crosses to wear representing homicide victims in Buffalo, as she had done the previous year. She promised she would.

That Good Friday–April 14, 2006–was to be the last day of Sister Karen's life. At noon, she joined about twenty folks in downtown Buffalo to pray the Stations of the Cross. We used various landmarks in the city to represent different moments in Christ's passion. For example, we met in front of the police station as we recalled Jesus' arrest, and we stood in front of the courthouse when we remembered how Jesus was sentenced to death.

Before we started, Sister Karen passed out crosses for us to wear around our necks, each cross naming a homicide victim from the previous year. She told me that she and her guys were up late making the crosses. One of the men helping with those crosses on Holy Thursday would murder her later that Friday night.

Photo by Patrick Nash

~ April 14, 2006 ~
Sister Karen prays during Stations of the Cross, Good Friday, the day of her death.

Ironically, when she became a homicide victim herself, Sister Karen's death brought even more attention to her mission to "stop the violence."

On the walk during her last Stations of the Cross, Sister Karen and I talked about the problem of homicides in Buffalo. I said I had heard that six in ten cases were never solved. She told me it was worse than that. She had been keeping a huge sign in the shape of a dove in front of Bissonette House indicating the number of days since the last homicide. Sister Karen mentioned more than twenty days had passed as of that Good Friday, and she always got nervous when the number of days was that large because she knew another homicide would happen soon.

Walking with Sister Karen on Good Friday and watching her with a cross around her neck and literally carrying a large wooden cross through the streets of downtown Buffalo are my last memories of her. In walking with her on Good Friday and learning other life lessons on Fridays with Sister Karen, I cannot help but see her life and death as part of Christ's Paschal Mystery, the mystery of death and resurrection.

MATTHEW SMITH, his wife Agnes, and their three children live in Amherst, New York. Matt has a masters in theology from Christ the King Seminary and is the coordinator of the Buffalo Catholic Worker.

A Few Examples of Activities by Interfaith Peace Network

Cecily Whiteford, Sister Karen and
Sister Marion Zimmer, SSJ attend Qur'an 55 event

Qur'an 55

In June 2005 Karen joined in support of the "Qur'an 55," sponsored by the Interfaith Peace Network of Western New York. Religious leaders and others gathered "in solidarity with our Muslim brothers and sisters to help heal the wounds caused by the atrocities against Qur'an."

Gathering in a public group, everyone walked to Talking Leaves Bookstore to purchase a copy of the Qur'an and pledged to show respect for this sacred book of faith. [IPN chose the number 55 because the church that posted the sign "the Koran needs Flushing" was reported to have "about 55 members."]

Interfaith Peace Network sponsors a billboard to continue Sister Karen's message

From left to right: Phil Rumore - president, Buffalo Teachers Federation; Sister Elizabeth Savage, former SSJ president, Congregation of Sisters of St. Joseph of Buffalo; Greg Brice, then executive director, Bissonette House; Patty DeVinney, field coordinator, WNY Area Labor Federation; Fr. Roy Herberger, pastor, SS. Columba–Brigid Church; Fr. Bob Gebhard - then pastor, St. James Church; Antoine Thompson, NYS Senator; Rev. Steve Phelps - then pastor, Central Presbyterian Church

90

Reflections of Peaceprints

Individual responses to Sister Karen

CENTER FOR
NONVIOLENCE

SSJ Sister Karen Klimczak

GARDEN of JOY

PAUL JENKINS
AGE 2?
MAY 27, 2007

The Wisest of Fools

Sister Ann Oestreich, IHM

Consider your calling, sisters and brothers. Not many of you were wise by human standards, not many were influential, and surely not many were well born. God chose those whom the world considers foolish … (I Cor. 1:26–27)

The Gospel message of justice and love was the motivating force in Karen's life. Sharing that message with others was her life's passion.

A master teacher, Karen always experimented with new techniques to get the message across to her students, children and adults alike. When she discovered the history and power of clowning, she found more than a new teaching technique. She found a way to help people not just to hear but to experience the gospel message in a new and deeper way. And she discovered an outlet for her considerable talents that was consistent with her spirituality.

Karen often said that in medieval times the clown or court jester was the one who went before the ruler to point out injustices and other situations that needed attention in the kingdom. Because the jester delivered the message in an entertaining and nonthreatening way, the ruler could receive the information that others in the reign might be afraid to deliver for fear of retribution. Knowing this, Karen thought clowning might be the perfect vehicle for helping people better understand and reflect on the Paschal [death and resurrection] mystery. For many people, the Cross seems to be the ultimate folly. Who better than a clown to propose another point of view?

Karen had been experimenting with clowning and sign language when she cajoled me into sharing this ministry with her. She thought that the interaction between two clowns would be more engaging, relational, and effective for communicating the message. So, I became Karen's student–and learned from her that clowning is serious business!

We worked hard on our prayer services–communicating a message without talking was a tremendous challenge. Each service was a nonverbal interaction between our "audience" and ourselves, interspersed with music, gesture, movement, and silence. The services came from two sources: our shared prayer and Karen's amazing creativity.

The prayer services were meticulously prepared and practiced. Every movement had a purpose. Our spiritual preparation was meticulous as well. We put on our costumes and make–up in silence. Karen believed that when we put on whiteface makeup, we were dying to ourselves. By using other colors (red noses, blue markings around our eyes, etc.) and costumes, we were becoming new persons. Preparing for clowning was a resurrection experience. We left our everyday selves behind and became new beings. The faces and the costumes helped define the new personalities we each assumed. During the time of prayer we became free to be who God wanted us to be. This "kairos moment" (holy or God–given time) was tangible–for us and for those who prayed with us. Our obvious transformation allowed others to open themselves to the mystery of grace, the Spirit, and a God who laughs and lives and loves us unconditionally.

Karen chose the perfect "clown name" for herself: Bounce. It described how free she was to "clown around with purpose." She took herself lightly, but never her clowning ministry.

As Bounce, Karen showed us that "God's foolishness is wiser than human wisdom" (I Cor. 1:25) and that in God's hands, Bounce was the wisest of fools.

All biblical quotes are taken from The Inclusive New Testament, published by Priests For Equality, Brentwood, Maryland, 1994.

SISTER ANN OESTREICH, IHM, *currently serves as the Congregation Justice Coordinator for the Sisters of the Holy Cross in Notre Dame, Indiana. She also serves on the board of directors of several justice organizations, including Jubilee USA Network and the Africa Faith and Justice Network in Washington, D.C. She and Sister Karen both taught at Mount Saint Joseph Academy and engaged in clown ministry in the late 1970s and early 1980s.*

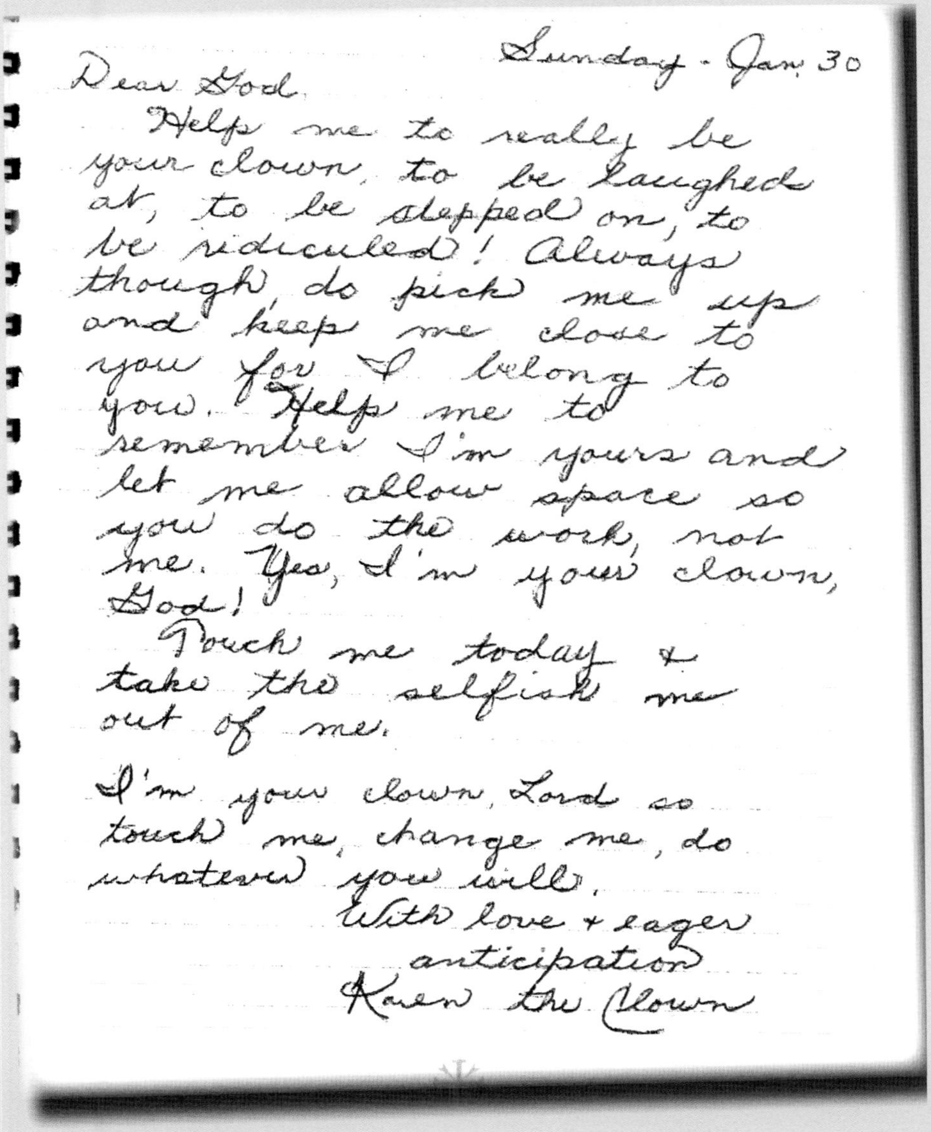

Sunday - Jan. 30

Dear God,

Help me to really be your clown, to be laughed at, to be stepped on, to be ridiculed! Always though, do pick me up and keep me close to you for I belong to you. Help me to remember I'm yours and let me allow space so you do the work, not me. Yes, I'm your clown, God!

Touch me today & take the selfish me out of me.

I'm your clown, Lord so touch me, change me, do whatever you will.

With love & eager
anticipation
Karen the Clown

Sister Karen as Bounce the clown

A Story of Clown Ministry from Sister Karen's Journal

Nov. 1, 1984

Listen to what I say.

... The water I give shall become a fountain within him, leaping up to provide eternal life.
(John 4:14)

My eyes were opened and I was able to see. They were opened by a legally blind girl. A legally blind girl was the Lord's instrument who was used to touch me. Yes, I decided I was going to dress up as a clown and visit the patients at Roswell [Roswell Park Cancer Institute]. As I began putting on my makeup, I felt very reluctant about doing it, but said, "Why, Lord, am I really doing this? Who are the persons that cry out to us for help? Is my heart open to them?"

Of course, I didn't bother waiting for an answer. Decided to start off in pediatrics and so I began my rounds. As I entered one room, a visitor for one of the children said that if I intend to visit the girl in bed with the curtain around it–just to let me know–the girl was legally blind. I thanked the woman and proceeded to knock on the curtain saying, "I'm a clown–can I come in?" "A clown," a girl of about eight squealed in reply, "oh, I love clowns–they're my favorite people. Come in. Oh, please, please come real close to me so I can see you."

As I came within a few inches of her face, she said, "Oh, you're a happy clown ... I love happy clowns ... never ever become a sad clown ... " My heart melted ... I made animal balloons for her and she felt them to guess what they were ... She squealed with delight as I handed her a strawberry scratch & sniff sticker for it was her favorite flavor and she happened to collect stickers ... When it was time to leave, she asked me for a kiss and said, "Please, please come back."

The next day I only had an hour between school and my next meeting, but I knew I just had to return–I put my clown suit & makeup in my backpack and biked down to the hospital–ran up to pediatrics–the nurses & Tammy's mom were excited–all night long that's all Tammy talked about was "the clown."

When I came in this time, Tammy asked me why my hair was red & yellow. (Close up the colors were obvious.) I explained to her that I was God's clown and the yellow stood for joy & red for love. As a clown, God asked me to touch others with His joy and His love. Then I pulled out a little stuffed red & yellow clown I had brought for her–She held it closely and exclaimed– "Oh, this is my love 'n joy clown. Whenever I meet anyone who is sad, I'm going to let them hold my clown and they'll become happy. And when I hurt or I am sad, I'm going to hold my clown close to me and ask God to make me happy." As I kissed Tammy good–bye, my tears joined hers. Yes, my eyes and heart were opened by a child who could not see.

Tammy died two days later in her own home holding on to a love 'n joy clown.

Editor's note: This story of clown ministry is not presented in Sister Karen's original handwriting because of its length.

A Conversation with Father Roy Herberger

Evelyn McLean Brady

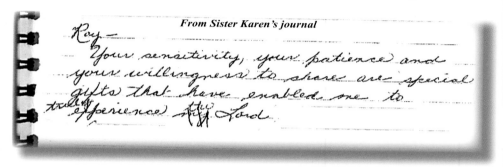

From Sister Karen's journal

Roy—
Your sensitivity, your patience and your willingness to share are special gifts that have enabled me to truly experience the Lord.

Evelyn: When I mentioned to Sister Jean [Karen's sibling] that I was going to interview you, she said, "They were blessed with a deep, spiritual friendship–like Francis and Clare." When she said this, I thought of how friends totally dedicated to spreading the Gospel can sustain each other through the difficult and daily challenges and support the deepest places of each other's hearts. These rare friends are gifts from God.

Sister Karen and Father Roy

Father Roy: Right from the very beginning there was definitely a bond between us. It was something deep, very real and very human. It was a beautiful friendship because it was so natural. You would never have found us talking about something like that. "Isn't this really wonderful, this deep relationship we have?" No, it was just there. I don't want to say it was taken for granted because that sounds negative. It was accepted and appreciated—so much so that no matter where I was assigned, Karen always wanted to show support for me. "What can I do to make it less of a burden for you, Roy? How can I help so you are not so overworked?"

Evelyn: What do you do when you lose someone so central to you, someone you love so dearly, someone who helped you in so many ways? What happens to you?

Father Roy: You get angry. You feel lost, empty, and for a while you just don't give a darn. You go through the motions and hope that the spark will come back. You're grateful for the support people offer and patient with prayer. A lot of times anything that just reminds me of Karen catches my breath, brings tears in my eyes, halting speech as they say. It varies from time to time. Then eventually you can start going again, start working again but saying, "What if Karen were here? What would she have done? How would she do this?"

Evelyn: You knew and worked with Karen for over twenty–five years. How did you meet?

Father Roy: We met in the 1980s while I was pastor at Our Lady of Lourdes and St. Boniface in downtown Buffalo. Sister Mary Pat Barth and Karen wanted to involve some Newman Club students who maybe would want to walk the journey of faith in a small, supportive community. It would be like an intentional Christian community—to have meals together, pray together, socialize together, and anytime questions or problems arose, we would be there for one another. The sisters asked if I would be open to housing the community at Our Lady of Lourdes rectory. So it came about: the two sisters, two male and two female students, and myself. It was really a wonderful experience being with younger people, idealistic, searching, questioning, just a wonderful blend. The community continued for a few years with new students coming in and out.

Evelyn: What could you say was most evident about Karen's spirit and her thinking at that time?

Father Roy: Whether it was with children in the school or college students at the house or parishioners at Lourdes, her questions were always the same: What are we all about? Where should we be at this point in our lives? What is the Gospel of Jesus Christ inviting us to or challenging us to do?

Evelyn: Was prison ministry part of her life then? How did she get involved with former prisoners?

Father Roy: Probably the Bedford Hills experience was pivotal. Every summer Karen would do some ministry when she wasn't teaching. She would be reaching out to others during the summertime—not just vacationing and relaxing! One year, for example, she went down to Atlanta, Georgia, where those children were murdered so she could work with the surviving children who were so traumatized. She brought Bounce, her clown life, to them.

A year or two later, in late spring, she realized there was only one option left for the summer ministry—prison ministry with women released from prison and their children in New York City. Her first reaction was, "Don't even think about me doing prison ministry. I would never fit in. I can't imagine what my family would say." But she wanted to do some summer ministry so she decided to work with women and their children at Providence House in Bedford Hills.

When that summer was over, Karen became increasingly interested in prison ministry in general. She was aware of the whole idea about incarcerated people being released with no place to go, being rejected by their families, and having no welcome in society. Who's going to hire them, how will they get jobs, etc.? She was thinking about all these concerns. It was that overall experience of seeing their fears, their frustrations, and their difficulties at the time of being released that affected her. Then, she took it to the next step.

She began saying, "One thing I know for sure; I have to get a house started for men when they come out of prison." I can remember telling her, "That's a great idea, Karen. But where are we going to get the money? What place are we going to find?" She didn't hesitate: "The Lord will lead me somehow, somewhere. The Lord wants it and the Lord will provide." The money wasn't going to be a problem for her. She went full speed ahead. Donations came in and different people were very much for the concept. She didn't say, "Let's take a year and have forty–two committee meetings and vote and discuss everything." No, it was, "We are going to do it." That's how deeply she trusted in the Lord.

Evelyn: She had so much energy.

Father Roy: That's it. She would set her mind and she would get things done. I mean, how she could put everybody to shame. She had that energy within her. She was biologically, physically, chemically blessed in a different way—much more energy than most people have. The Lord truly blessed her even in that way. I am unable to describe her, except to say that she was running on all cylinders, all the time. For the most part, that lack of vacation time, space, quiet, up to a certain point, didn't really deeply affect her in a negative way, because she always had this energy.

Evelyn: Father Joe Bissonette was a central person in Karen's life. What could you say about how Father Joe influenced Karen?

Father Roy: Very honestly, what has been said about Joe is what we are now saying about Karen. Joe was another Christ working in our midst. Joe was someone who taught us how to forgive. He was someone who literally would turn the other cheek. He was a priest who really lived the Gospel, not just in light of his death. She had this great admiration for him and appreciation for him. That is why Karen saw what would become Bissonette House—not just the house but the whole area—as sacred ground, holy ground.

Evelyn: Even though Karen was part of a religious community, she had an autonomous sense about her. She exhibited an independent energy.

Father Roy: Oh, she was definitely independent, even within her religious community. It shows how she relied on the power of prayer, the presence of the Holy Spirit in her, God working in a person. The Sisters of St. Joseph have a wonderful reputation for putting themselves "out there" for people. But one of their own, living alone, by herself, with nine men, ex–offenders? That took a lot of faith and courage on their part. When she went to ask permission to have a halfway house for former inmates, Karen feared that logic would win over faith. But faith won. Her community gave her permission.

Evelyn: Faith. Could you talk about what kind of prayer life sustained Karen?

Father Roy: She herself found her greatest strength in meditative, reflective prayer rather than a community prayer–by herself, just walking or riding a bicycle, journaling or camping, but in silence, in reflection, letting as much as possible just be put aside. Then she could just concentrate and listen to God speak to her. And she would talk to God: "Lord, am I doing what you want me to do? Am I headed in the direction that you have planned for me? What do I need to learn? What do I need to change?" Her deepest prayer, I would say, was the individual, deep, reflective, contemplative kind of prayer.

Prayer was so important for her at the house and making sure that every single resident knew that his prayer was just as good, just as important as her prayer. She believed we have to go beyond what is Catholic or non–Catholic and remember that we reach out to all.

From Sister Karen's journal

Sept 28, 1984
Friday

I really feel that the community would support me in my endeavors to set up a home for ex-offenders. Lord, I feel so drawn to all of this & yet at the same time I feel so frightened by all of it. Be with me – Let me keep my eyes on You. I love You and want to follow You so much. Somehow I truly feel You are & will be with me — You will not fail me.

Evelyn: Tell me about what she did here at SS. Columba–Brigid Church.

Father Roy: When I started here as pastor, the first opportunity was for a teen center. Karen and I talked about the need of bringing both the African–American and the Hispanic youth together in a safe place. That was really the initial involvement. Of course, after the church fire in 2004, she was very involved helping me come up with designs and ideas. "Don't forget we need classrooms; we better expand this; what are we going to do about that big window?" She wouldn't call herself a pastoral associate. "I'm just here to help. I don't want a title." She was not big on titles or recognition, but she literally became our right hand and left hand and everything else. She'd always joked, "What's my ministry, again?" It didn't really matter to her—whatever the need might be as long as she was helping. She was the kind of person who not only came up with the ideas or a challenge *for* me, but then she would do it! It was never, "Okay, go for it. I gave you the idea, and now you do the work." No, she did more than anyone. It is almost like a plant that is growing. A little seed with the teen center, a shoot here with liturgy, a shoot there with the parish council, another shoot there with lectors and Eucharistic ministers. Just this huge bush, using the symbolism of the mustard seed in the Gospel that all these birds, all these people could come to this haven of Columba–Brigid, could come and feel protected and at home.

101

Evelyn: In the last couple of years before her death, I felt another movement within Karen, a letting go, like nothing mattered but the stemming of violence. She looked very weary and very tired.

Father Roy: Yes. I think all of it took a toll on Karen in those last couple of years; so much so, it wasn't difficult to get her to take a day off. She really saw she had to do it or she wouldn't have been able to go on.

Nonviolence was her primary focus. More and more her concern was on the fact that she could not understand or accept all this ridiculous violence, overwhelming drive–by shootings, stabbings. It really got to her especially when young people were victims or some elderly woman who had been living there for eighty years was raped, robbed, and murdered. Her question was always, "How can I be an instrument of peace or voice for peace?"

I saw restlessness in her. First the initial sign, "NONVIOLENCE begins with ME!" Then coming up with this other idea, "I Leave PEACEPRINTS." She was always thinking, "How am I going to do it? I just know I have to do it. I don't know how it's going to work out, but it will work out, whether in high schools or with younger kids, but somehow we've got to get the message of nonviolence out." It was a compulsion, a real drive. That was very much where her heart was, and it drove her ministry the few years before she died.

Evelyn: What would you say is the impact of Karen on your own life in your role as a priest, as a pastor, as a minister to the poor?

Father Roy: I just know I was so blessed to have someone like her in my life. One of the things that really hit me hard at her death was thinking about the people who never will have met her, never will be touched by her example, her love, her selflessness, and so I feel bad for people I do not even know for not having known her.

But I would hope, like Karen, that I could be the kind of person who would respond to the Gospel however, wherever, whenever. I would hope that, like Karen, I will always see love in all people, so it is a reality check … a reminder because a lot of this stuff … I have always been working on. So it's not something totally new.

But seeing it in her, experiencing it with her, that gave me more opportunity to do more of the same. Not to give up on certain principles, on certain values, certain outlooks. If I am feeling sorry for myself, I think of Karen. I can hear her saying, "Right–come on, Roy, get with it and get out there and make that phone call, go ahead and go to that meeting or whatever." Her example is always before me and I'm conscious of it, and so I have one less excuse for not being who I'm supposed to be.

HARRY SCULL JR/The Buffalo News

Father Roy Herberger preaches forgiveness at Sister Karen's funeral.

From Sister Karen's journal

Where am I as an SSJ of Bflo?

What would I personally like
to pass on~

call to be freer / to let go...
self most huet~ closed off self...
let go of what is dying—
Greater freedom in God

Hopefully—
I am at a point of
wanting to RISK and
RESPOND —— to the
drawings of the Spirit
in my Life ——

Corporate Commitment
Sisters of St. Joseph of Buffalo

In our desire to bring about
unity and reconciliation,
and out of our deep reverence for all life,
we, the Sisters of St. Joseph
and Associates of Buffalo,
make a corporate commitment
to confront violence and powerlessness
in ourselves and in our society.

November 1996

Easter Week 2006

Sister Elizabeth Savage, SSJ

Early morning phone calls on Sunday seldom brought me casual questions. That Easter Sunday was no exception. "What's happened to Karen Klimczak?" made no sense—until I turned on the TV, saw her picture, and heard that she was missing. It all seemed impossible. And it began a week like no other, a week that has become part of my mind and heart and very bones.

What was it like? So often, it was like walking a tightrope In the early hours, I had hope that Karen was safe—and fear that she was being held somewhere. As I responded to the media's questions, I could feel myself torn. Would my words put her in further danger or rather convey my desire to let her know of my and the congregation's support of her? As the hours went on, with the police and representatives from parole becoming more involved, it grew harder to balance the increasing likelihood that her situation was critical and my hope that such was not the case.

With the news of Karen's disappearance spreading locally, the phone was seldom quiet. People needed information; I had questions. My feelings could not be central. That evening, as I called other Sisters of St. Joseph congregations asking for prayers, was another story. Just hearing myself say, "One of our Sisters is missing," reduced me to tears born of fear. My calls after Karen's body was found likewise came amid tears, tears of sorrow and a certain relief. Hard as it was, the terrible waiting was over.

What was it like? It was a tremendous call to sensitivity. As a Sister of St. Joseph, Karen had placed herself at the service of others through the way she had been called to live out our mission and, in particular, our Corporate Commitment. That way—director of Bissonette House and tremendous involvement in many aspects of prison and parish ministry—had made her a very public person. She was also a vibrant part of the large, loving Klimczak family. As president of the congregation, I fielded a multitude of questions and constantly felt the need to take many others into consideration in making decisions and plans.

What was it like? There were so many moments of gratitude. So often during those days I experienced a very personal sense of God's providence: I was at home to respond to the situation in the name of the Sisters of St. Joseph. Had the plans I had arranged a year before materialized, I would have been traveling that Easter Sunday, returning from vacation. Moving the date of that vacation up two weeks was hard when I needed to reschedule. I was so grateful I had made the change. With the entire Western New York community, I shared the tremendous relief that Karen's body was found as soon as it was. The two days of not having her seemed endless; I can only guess the pain of those who must wait weeks or months to have a missing loved one found.

Our Sisters and Associates, Karen's family, close colleagues, and residents of Bissonette House needed a private opportunity to share their grief and to pray. We welcomed them to a liturgy and brunch at our Clarence residence. With Karen's Mass of Christian Burial set for April 22, demands for planning and decisions again grew. Representing the congregation amid the hundreds who filled St. Ann Church for the funeral was almost overwhelming. Often during that liturgy, and often since, I drew support from the special moment I had shared—a very private viewing of Karen just prior to her cremation. Blessing her body, giving her a good—by kiss—these brought a calm. She was peaceful; she was beautiful; she was home.

Karen's message "I Leave PEACEPRINTS" resounded through St. Ann Church the morning of her funeral. My prayer then, and since, is that our lives will speak that message—a message reflecting one Sister of St. Joseph's way of living out our Corporate Commitment.

SISTER ELIZABETH SAVAGE, SSJ, *was president of the Sisters of St. Joseph of Buffalo at the time of Sister Karen's murder.*

HARRY SCULL JR/The Buffalo News

Sister Karen's funeral at St. Ann Church

Sisters of St. Joseph and Associates Remember Their Sister, Karen Klimczak, SSJ

Nothing Stopped Her

Sister Marian Schwenk, SSJ

Back in the late 1970s, I had the privilege of living with Karen and will never forget the night she went out to walk to a meeting after dinner. Not long after she left, there was a pounding on the front door and an urgent ringing of the doorbell.

Upon opening the door, we found Karen gasping for breath and exhausted. When she was finally able to speak, she told of being grabbed by a man about a block away and of struggling to free herself from him. She then ran all the way home.

After catching her breath, she insisted on starting out again - on foot. This is just one example of how fearless and how full of trust she was in her dedication to her ministry.

Should I Be Doing This?

Sister John Maron Abdella, SSJ

In the early days of Sister Karen's work running HOPE House as a residence for recently paroled men, she came to see me. "People, even some sisters in our community are saying that I shouldn't be doing this, that it's too dangerous, that it's not appropriate. I really feel that this is what God is calling me to do, but I don't know how to deal with other people's concerns."

I could only share with her what has governed my own life: "If it truly is 'of God,' it will work out all right and their concerns will be laid to rest. God will give you the strength, and whatever He wills will be accomplished."

As I Knew Her

Sally Tower, SSJ Associate

ENERGY –
> **electricity, friction, heat, potential, dynamic, service**

GOSPEL WOMAN –
> **healer, reconciler, crusader, unifier, compassionate Fool for God**

MENTOR and FRIEND –
> **guide, practitioner, cheerleader, challenger, supporter**

This is the Karen Klimczak I knew—a woman of energy, a Gospel woman, a mentor, and a friend. She had a very personal relationship with her God and that relationship guided her actions. Karen was a real human being, a woman of the twentieth and twenty–first centuries. She knew her gifts and her limitations and responded as best she could to further the "KINDOM" of God at this time and in this place.

Depth and Passion

Sister Rita Kane, SSJ

I taught with Karen in the 1980s at Mount Saint Joseph Academy. Karen was an alive, alert, ace teacher. She not only had a personal impact on each person she taught but also made a strong connection with each student's family. Karen never looked for honors or glory but focused her energy on her own simple little classroom.

I never appreciated the depth of her spirituality and her passion to live the Gospel message. I truly regret that I didn't know her better.

Feeding and Welcoming

Sister Veronica Anne Armao, SSJ

During her high school years at Immaculata Academy, Theresa Klimczak (later Sister Karen) volunteered after school to help feed the infants at Our Lady of Victory Infant Home in Lackawanna, New York. She was so reliable, dedicated, and had a great love for all the little ones. This included a very happy spirit which spread to all staff members in the Holy Angels Unit.

Theresa had such a welcoming spirit that she was hired to answer the door at the Infant Home when families came to visit with their children in the evenings. The memory of this spirit has always remained with me. Her smiling face and cheerful disposition brightened many days for me.

Clowning Around

Sister Philip Marie Cirincione, SSJ

In 1981, in the early years of Karen's religious life with the Sisters of St. Joseph, she did a lot of "clowning around" at the former St. Boniface Church located in the fruit belt of Buffalo. She was always available to attend our summer vacation Bible School classes as well as our Saturday spiritual program. The message of the Lord came so alive with her that children and young people always responded positively.

Karen also loved to paint clown faces on the children in our newly formed St. Martin de Porres Parish and in our neighborhood. She was active in our National Night Out program, where the young people just made themselves "at home" with her.

In the House with Karen

Judy Major, SSJ Associate

I was doing graduate work at Christ the King Seminary and met Karen in 1991 when I did my field education experience for one year at HOPE House. My duties were varied: visiting men in prison who were going to become residents, helping to teach the residents food preparation, driving residents to appointments and listening to their stories—but "being there" and having time for them was the most important aspect of my responsibilities. That same year Karen asked me to be a member of the board of directors for HOPE House. In 1998, I became Karen's administrative assistant.

Karen not only believed in Jesus, but she lived Jesus' Gospel message. When I think of Karen, I see her embracing the Beatitudes. She would often visit inmates in the prisons or in the hospital. Families of inmates could count on her support when their loved ones were in Erie County Medical Center. She would set up housing, transportation, and visitation for them. Neighbors sometimes asked for food from the house, and we shared whatever we could. What touched me about Karen was her boundless energy and willingness to help all in need, including me. She was there for my outpatient surgeries and when my mother was dying.

Her inability to see color or race was remarkable. All the men were accepted as equals and as her brothers. Material goods were not important to Karen. Our energy needed to be spent in helping others, in bringing about peace. It is no wonder she forgave her killer even before he committed the act. That was Karen's way.

A Big Beautiful Tree

Gerry Neff, SSJ Associate

I first met Karen Klimczak in the early 1980s. We worked bingo together, and she taught two of my children at Mount St. Joseph Elementary School. Karen was a bundle of energy and responded to God's call by promoting human dignity centered on her belief in Jesus.

As I reflect on our friendship, I think of Karen as a big beautiful tree. The trunk of the tree is Karen's charisma with peace flowing to each branch.

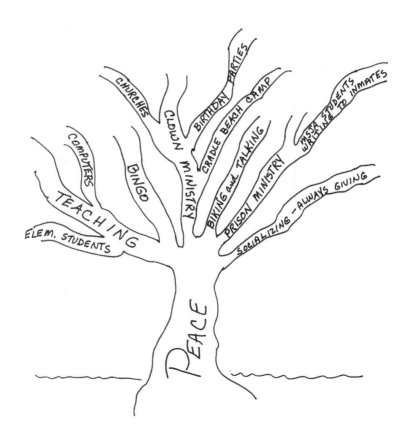

Journeying Together
Sister Mary Jo Colucci, SSJ

When Karen and I lived together after her transfer into our SSJ community, I was asked to accompany her on her spiritual journey. We met to share prayer on a regular basis, and it was a grace–filled time for me to experience her creative prayer journey.

On one occasion, Karen drew some of her prayer ideas on paper. She created the word "YES," but the "Y" was made in a different way. The top part was more of a "U" shape that then became a representation of arms upraised. A little circle was placed in the middle of the "U" representing a head, so that the letter "Y" looked like a person praying with arms extended to God.

The word "YES" then became a symbol for reaching up to God with openness and joy. That's the way I always thought of Karen. Her life was always a "YES" to God and that became obvious to all of us who knew and loved her. It's a memory I cherish and which reminds me of how important a focus that is in living my own life.

The Peace Book of One Red Triangle
Bennett Park Montessori
in honor of Sister Karen.

(Barbara Faust, teacher)

Samples of pages in the Peace Book.

"Peace is having new friends and letting them visit your heart," said Paloma.

"Peace is a gentle bird making a nest," said Marilinn.

Teaching by Example

"You can do it!"

Julianna Ricci

"Highly creative, highly organized, and driven." Those were the qualities that stood out in Sister Bea Manzella's mind as she remembered the years when she lived and worked most closely with Sister Karen. "Karen was a mite of a woman, a spitfire," comments Sister Bea, "and

the finest possible example of the Sisters of St. Joseph's guiding principle of Ignation spirituality, always striving for 'the more.'" Karen was full of a swirling energy yet never surrounded by chaos. She was deeply drawn to the open classroom concept at Mt. St. Joseph Academy, where she taught for several years in the 1980s. Within the highly individualized program

Sister Bea Manzella, Mt. St. Joseph, and Sister Karen, circa 1980

that she created, Karen's space was totally organized and even color–coded. There was a sense of security in her middle–school classroom. Students were grouped according to their achievement levels; every level was encompassed by her belief: "You can do it! Trust me, follow me, and you will do it!" Karen's expectations were always clear and always lofty. She didn't use a lot of words, didn't "homilize" at the children, according to Sister Bea, but with a look, a gesture, communicated to her students what was expected.

Sometimes her vision of what could be, and the above–average expectations that accompanied it, could get in Karen's way. Because she was a complex human being and an unusually talented teacher, Karen walked the extra mile toward success and believed that others were perfectly capable of doing the same. Unfortunately, not all those "others" agreed with her, and sometimes they resisted her persistent positive attitude. She was particularly conscious of the boys she taught. They were a challenge to her but also familiar territory since Karen grew up with two sisters and nine brothers. Surely Karen's strength and determination derived at least in part from her early family experiences with her parents and siblings. Sister Bea remembers Karen's mother as a "beautiful, accepting woman of faith" and how Karen, no matter how tired or busy she was, would find time to visit her mother when she was a resident in the infirmary of the Sisters of St. Joseph.

A learning center in Sister Karen's classroom

Sister Bea knew Karen was a very private person, so it is difficult to say if she ever had doubts about her teaching or, later, her prison ministry. In Sister Bea's memory, Karen was ever confident, self-possessed, and never a "downer or in a dark space." To recharge, Karen spent time alone. She was a contemplative and would quietly disappear, even go camping alone to nourish herself in the natural world and in solitary communion with God. Her life wasn't the conventional life within a religious community; her community was wherever God called her to be. In some sense she was "a woman on the fringe."

Whatever Karen did, she was fully committed to that work and gave her full self to the energy center which claimed her. So sure of her path was she that some people might misread her single–mindedness as stubbornness or closed–mindedness. It is true that Karen pursued in her own way her vocation of education as she did her vision of how to promote nonviolence. Yet she supported "her way" with information, research, and action. She was as aware of the necessity for outreach to the larger, outside world as she was sensitive to the interior learning styles and modalities of her students within her classroom. Wherever she was, she moved instinctively to reach out to people where they were.

"When I think of Karen after all these years of knowing her, I remember her distinctive artistic style—in her printing, in her arrangement of space, in her ability to take an idea beyond what others might, even in her clowning ministry," says Sister Bea, "Karen was always searching, never satisfied with what is."

Karen made her mark on those she taught. She left her peaceprints.

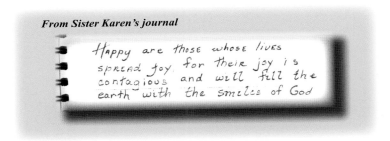

From Sister Karen's journal

Happy are those whose lives
spread joy, for their joy is
contagious and will fill the
earth with the smiles of God

JULIANNA RICCI, a retired teacher of English, is a poet, writer, and painter of icons in the Eastern Orthodox tradition. Julie enjoys volunteering with Meals on Wheels and at the Albright-Knox Art Gallery as a docent, but being with her three daughters and their families is her greatest joy.

From Sister Karen's journal

freedom
the "EACHNESS"

To be a dandelion
To let go...
To know he will
be there to
catch me...
to mold me...
for He loves me...

Woman of Peace, Agent of Change: Living the Gospel

Steve Banko

I have vivid, if not always fond, memories of boyhood in Holy Family parish in South Buffalo. Between the *Baltimore Catechism* and altar boy duties, I was imbued with the theory of Catholicism, but not the reality. In those days, I would frequently wear out the knees of my pants in fervent and various supplications praying to God, Jesus, the Virgin Mother, St. Jude, or any other of the sanctified. Invariably, I was using prayer to try to change the world around me, to try to make that world conform to my desires. I had not yet understood that prayer changes us, not the world. It changes our relationship with the world and the people in our universe. We change and in changing are called to change the world.

I still hadn't learned that lesson when I went to war. My failure to learn and to understand frequently led me to the brink of despair. I wanted my prayer to be like a magic carpet, wafting me away from the carnage and the suffering. When my prayers didn't remove me from the inferno, I began to doubt my faith as I wondered if the terrible silence that answered my prayers was, indeed, the voice of God—a God unconcerned with my suffering and oblivious to the bloodshed around me. I wanted my circumstance changed even as I ignored my obligation to be an agent of that change. Slowly, the lesson of what I should be praying for surrounded me. It got great stimulus when a young man literally sacrificed his life to save mine. He recognized that it was for him to change the world around him, not for the world to be changed. He saw my need. He responded to that need. He gave his life to preserve mine.

And so it was that I saw saintliness in the world for the first time. No longer did I need the catechism or the biographies of long–ago saints to teach me. I was surrounded by the blood, death, and suffering of war and I saw the face of a saint. It was contorted with pain. It was covered in blood. It reflected the understanding that life would end in that terrible inferno. It also reflected the desire of this young man to be the change he sought in the world. He took the risk at the cost of his life and, in so doing, he gave life to me.

Almost forty years later, I saw that sainthood again. I saw it in the face of Sister Karen Klimczak. I didn't know Sister Karen and, indeed, never even met her. But having seen humanity at its best, one never fails to recognize the aura of that humanity again. Karen was not a woman who only prayed for peace. She was not a woman who only prayed for deliverance. She was not a woman who only prayed for change. She was a woman who would be peace, who would be deliverance, who would be change for so many criminals and ex–offenders on whom society had turned its collective back. In a world increasingly populated by spectators, Sister Karen was a participant. She was one of those people who had to be in the game, not just in the arena. She saw a need and tried to fill it. She saw pain and tried to relieve it. She saw despair and tried to infuse it with new hope. What more could life be?

My life has been anything but dull. Legend assigns a curse in Chinese lore that says, "May you live in interesting times." I have frequently wished my "times" might not have been quite so interesting. One such time was in Cheektowaga town court when our son was led into court in shackles around his wrists, waist, and ankles. No pain that ever befell me in Vietnam could match that pain. In the end, though, my son had a loving family that refused to give up on him. Our family also had resources to bring to bear in the fight to rehabilitate him. I began to think about what other offenders had and, more importantly, didn't have in their struggles. How impossible must it be for so many men and women to recover from addictions and the criminal histories attendant with those addictions?

And all the while I was thinking about it, Sister Karen was doing something about it. She was opening eyes to the plight of people trying to put their lives back together. She didn't just pray for these people. She held out her life as her prayer. She worked tirelessly. She gave continually. She loved unconditionally. If her experience was like our own, the disappointments far outnumbered the victories. But she persevered as if to tell those she cared for that as long as they tried, they had her to rely on. She transformed "peace" from a noun into an active verb. In her life, peace was not an abstraction, not a dream. The rosary might have been the typical tool for nuns praying for kids like me, but Sister Karen used peace as a tool to care for the hardened, the disenfranchised, and the discarded among us.

Recent revelations about Mother Teresa's doubts and despair in the face of human suffering made me wonder if Sister Karen encountered the same doubts. It is hard to imagine that she didn't, given the role she chose to play among society's outcasts. But just as Teresa's "dark nights of the soul" make her work even more luminous, so would they emphasize Karen's commitment to the gospel of love. Having foreseen her own betrayal and her own death at the hands of one of those she loved so much, Karen's enduring legacy was that she didn't quit her mission. She knew, and still she did.

In doing so, she showed us that our most effective prayers change us so that we can change our world. Lord, let me be an instrument of Thy peace.

Once tormented by memories of war, **STEVE BANKO** *now comforts himself and his community with dreams of peace. He also writes a monthly column for the St. Ambrose Parish newsletter.*

Sister Karen

Sister Meg Quinlan, RSM

For anyone who was murdered
or caught in a crossfire
or a drive–by
or some other senseless killing,
Karen called together whoever would come.

You who died here
your life mattered
and you too who hunted, hide.
A simple prayer for mercy
for the killer and the killed
for the families of both
and for all who, wounded, watch.

Now she is with Romero
and Maura and Jean,
with Ita and Dorothy
and David and Joe
our heroes

disappeared.

April 20, 2006

Photo – George Schaeffer

My Neighbor, Sister Karen

A Conversation with Rev. Jeff Carter

Lillis McLean

Lillis: Ephesus Ministries has a deep connection with Sister Karen. Can you tell me about your church and its mission?

Rev. Carter: Actually, Karen is the reason we are in this particular space, the site of the former St. Bartholomew Church where Karen's great friend Father Joe Bissonette was the pastor. When I retired as chaplain from Attica Correctional Facility, I recognized that I couldn't retire entirely from ministry. I was moved to start a new church, from the ground up. Karen said, "Jeff, why don't you come over and take the building next door so we can continue doing ministry together?" Somehow that's the way it worked out. We chose Ephesus Ministries for our name because when St. Paul went to Ephesus, he did evangelization—promoted the Gospels. We focus on touching lives with the love of Christ. That is who we are. My concept of ministry is not just a space for worship but a way to *do* ministry. Doing ministry outside the church doors is what Karen was all about. Karen even had a key to our social hall. She was in and out of this place all the time, and my members saw her as one of us.

Lillis: Ephesus Ministries has donated part of your space for the SSJ Sister Karen Klimczak Center for Nonviolence. Does the church have any role with the Center?

Rev. Carter: We don't necessarily see it as "donating space" for the Center. We see it as a part of who we are, and we are so happy that the Sisters of St. Joseph would allow us to be a part of what they are doing. We believe they are a part of who we are. So it's not really donating space; it is just good that we can be together in ministry.

Lillis: Karen educated us and kept us aware of the ongoing tragedy of violence, personal and systemic. What, in your view, should our churches and community do in practical ways to stem the violence around us?

Rev. Carter: In a practical way, every person in every church and in every community has to touch one life at a time. We have to keep doing what Karen did, educating people, talking to people, and speaking out against the violence. I believe that wherever there is darkness, each candle that is lit dispels the darkness around it. We just have to keep on, one person at a time, lighting those candles. Maybe we will never totally get rid of the darkness, but every little bit of light dispels some of the darkness. Karen knew about light. At the Remembering and Pledging service held at Ephesus each July, Karen had a candle lit for every victim of violence in the previous year, and she helped start the candlelight vigils at homicide sites. Those vigils mean so much to people who have lost someone to violence, but they are also significant for others who go and stand there and pray with the grieving families. Every time we do this, someone gains hope.

Hope says that God really does hear us. It is hope that says somehow in all of the senseless violence, in all of the pain, there is still some good. Every time a voice cries and a candle is lit out there, a little bit of hope is present.

Lillis: What does Karen's life teach us now?

Rev. Carter: Some people believe that angels have halos and wings. I believe that angels are messengers that God sends to give us a message. As a matter of fact, when you read about angels in the Bible, they appear suddenly to leave a message of change, and then, almost as suddenly as they appear, they are gone. To me Karen was an angel. She came with all the power of God, she gave us a life–changing message, and suddenly she was gone. It is very painful because Karen's death is a great loss for us. But I think in a very godly sense, it was not only the message that she brought, but even in her leaving suddenly, that she left such a worth. The impact of Karen's life remains with us, and it grows and continues to grow more each day. It was a life that wasn't just here and gone, but a life that has just grown greater in magnitude in her absence.

Lillis: Karen's life lives on.

Rev. Carter: Yes, Karen's life lives on. It lives on not only in the SSJ Sister Karen Klimczak Center for Nonviolence but in all the people who continue to so fervently carry out her work and vision. Just today, a young man pulled up in his truck and asked to purchase one of the peaceprint lawn signs. Every person who puts one of Karen's signs in their yard or wherever people can see it, the message of nonviolence, the message of peace will continue to spread. Every time the message spreads, it does a little bit more to stop the violence.

Photo – George Schaeffer

Angel statue in Sister Karen's Peace Garden

LILLIS McLEAN, *a former social worker with the Buffalo Public Schools, enjoys her involvement with the American Association of University Women, a local garden club, and her volunteer work with refugees. She also appreciates time at her cottage where she entertains the McLean family's next generation of little ones.*

The Moral Compulsion to Act

... like faith, knowledge without action is dead.

Peter K.B. St. Jean, Ph.D.

It is my strong belief that, like faith, knowledge without action is dead. We have the moral imperative to translate knowledge, interests, and curiosity into action. My work and study regarding the causes, consequences, and potential solutions to violence—especially those that lead to homicides in our society—would not have had sufficient footing if many individuals and organizations had not supported my practice to transform knowledge into action.

It is through the action of helping to solve real-world problems, with real-world people, in real-world situations that knowledge takes on true meaning. Therefore, my knowledge gained through those engagements with world problems and my work in concert with others who are serious about resolving them was not my own. Instead, such knowledge belongs to the very people whose suffering gave meaning to the interests, curiosity, and subsequent knowledge that emerged from gaining trust and even from prying into their lives. I realize I have a moral compulsion or obligation to share my knowledge with these people, many of whom have lenses that are too obscured by the circumstances of their suffering to see the light of this knowledge.

It is also my obligation to share this knowledge in such a way that persons, who are either unaware or not sufficiently aware of the truth of those conditions that perpetuate violence, should become enlightened—but enlightened in such a way that they also become committed to tangible, practical, and sustainable action. It is not enough to feed the hungry. Through sharing knowledge, we need to help people better understand why they are hungry and how to do more for themselves so that they too enjoy the dignity of independence. This same knowledge must be shared with others who are honest about helping. If we do not develop a compulsion to act in this manner, our efforts will only continue to glorify us and line our pockets. That, to me, would be a travesty.

After I gave a recent speech on this topic, a gentleman came up to me and said he had never heard anyone else address what he had been taught by the St. Vincent Brothers: service as a privilege. That conversation reminded me of my interactions with another person who believed service was privilege, Sister Karen Klimczak, someone with whom I had brief and intense encounters for about sixteen months.

I first met Sister Karen in November 2004 at a community event, but my first interaction with her was in the summer of 2005 after she came to one of our Stop the Violence Coalition meetings at the United Way. She attended the meeting as part of her campaign to have her NONVIOLENCE begins with ME! signs posted on lawns all over the city. She wanted to send the message that we are all responsible for the violence in our city and that we can take action to make a difference, but the difference really has to begin with our own actions.

now Paul. She wonders if she is being punished. Veronica laments that the newspaper implied he was a thug. Still, the Buffalo Common Council declared June 7, 2007, "Paul Jenkins, Jr. Day," in memory of the young man who was such a strong, positive force among peers and family. She elaborates, calling up a good–natured, funny, loving, generous young man, a hub who helped keep everyone around him upbeat, an equal to his father in how he liked everybody and judged no one.

When his friends had an "attitude" about a family member, he made them laugh and change their minds, as if he was their brother or father or uncle. He never went out much because they all came to her house to hang out and play video games. Despite his death, they still come and Veronica doesn't stop them. Sometimes they can't look her in the eye. In his memory, his friends acquired tattoos that read "Prince of Peace." Even so, Veronica needs to remind them that he can't be brought back by retaliation; that they need to "use that energy in a positive way." She admonishes his little cousins, who relied on Paul to take them for haircuts or wherever else they needed to go, that Paul wouldn't want them to be angry or upset, that his presence had been a blessing.

She confides, "I put all of my love and trust in Paul, when I think God wanted me to put all my love and trust in Him, instead." Were she to ask God something, she would simply ask Him to have mercy on her.

When she met Paul's father, he was a gambler, lying around all day and going out at night. The time came, Veronica says, when she told him to leave because she didn't want Paul learning from his example. "Well," she laughs, "he got up off his crutch, got his own apartment, even bought a bicycle for Paul and was always helping somebody out. So eventually we started messing around together again." Like Paul, he had tried to teach her that loving wasn't enough; they both wanted her to *like* everyone. He and Paul are Veronica's angels now, whispering to her to find the good in people, to move on.

With the loss of her job Veronica lost the insurance policy she had for Paul. Otherwise, there would be money for his girl and their daughter. Instead of the "big old wedding" she wanted for them, now Veronica is faced with making sure that his child is provided for. She thinks about throwing a baby shower with a Chinese auction to raise money to help mother and child get off to a good start. She looks at photographs, places them with care in a book for Paul's baby, desiring her grandchild to know the kind of person he was.

Three o'clock is when Paul came in from work. This is when Veronica tries to keep busy. She is reaching out so her loss doesn't fester, keen "to embrace and encourage people to help themselves and do good." A major goal is to start up a foundation to help meet the needs of families of murder victims. She will concentrate on helping others. Meanwhile, Veronica is setting boundaries with family members addicted to drugs and alcohol—who provide her with more to forgive.

Veronica's son, Paul Jenkins Jr.

She likes the Alternatives to Violence workshops and finds that, without aggression, any situation is easier to deal with. The Sister Karen Center, where Veronica does some volunteering, is a refuge for her, an oasis of peace and a sign of hope amid harsh realities in a large section of the city many people do their best to avoid.

Veronica thinks Sister Karen, if she were still here, could tell her how to go about some things, show her what to do. Seeing all the goodness around her, despite the crazy destructiveness that continues to erupt, she believes in her potential for being a blessing to someone else. If she is able to make it easier for people who want to make their lives better, she will. She is doing it for herself. Step by step, and in faith, she gets up in the morning, picks up the pieces of her life and goes on. Slowly, painfully, Veronica is beginning to heal. In the process, she is doing her part to alter society for the better. There is a fire in her, a glow in her eyes, an occasional winning smile. Sister Karen's life was a spark that lit the kindling. Veronica aims to keep it burning.

MARY O'HERRON, an addictions counselor and art therapist, mother and grandmother, is a member of a writers group and a meditation group. She lives with her husband, Brian, in Buffalo, where she maintains a flourishing urban garden.

From Sister Karen's journal

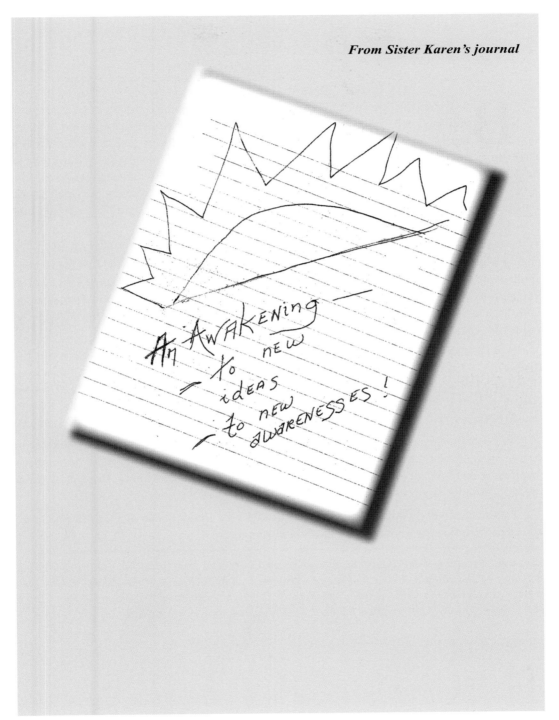

Her Narrow Path

Bill Marx

"Blessed are the peacemakers" is an invitation to us all, but how many of us are blessed with having had an opportunity to see that invitation fulfilled in the person of Sister Karen? To discover the gospel of nonviolence as I did very late in my life through Pax Christi USA, the Catholic peace movement, and then to come to know Sister Karen has to be defined as a very special invitation to find that narrow path of nonviolence that Jesus calls us to follow. I was gifted with a private lunch with the woman who lovingly provided a path for former inmates to return to society and whose dedication was often their first experience of God's love.

It was at that very informal "bite to eat" together that Sister Karen shared her dream of adding a resource center on nonviolence to Bissonette House: a corner office where anyone could come and find the stories and tools about peace and nonviolence too often hidden from us in our work–a–day world. We shared that dream but found ourselves immersed in our separate ministries to the exclusion of seeing such a sorely needed facility established in her lifetime. As the saying goes, "If you want God to laugh, tell Him your plans."

Now, thanks to the commitment and generosity of Sister Karen's religious community, the Sisters of St. Joseph and their Associates, God's plan has come into existence a few steps from Bissonette House. The SSJ Sister Karen Klimczak Center for Nonviolence, located on Durham Avenue behind Ephesus Cathedral, is a living monument to the dream of the anointed woman whose "Peaceprints" continue to be felt far beyond the borders of our City of Good Neighbors.

As I continue my "after–retirement–ministry" to establish a peace and justice committee in every parish of the Catholic Diocese of Buffalo, I work in a spirit of gratitude for having been inspired by that loving person of nonviolence, servant of the poor and the captives, incarnation of God's promise that peace is possible and that love changes everything.

These are merely words. Knowing Sister Karen was a prayer. Her example is a treasure beyond description for which I thank the God of Abraham.

A retired president of the Better Business Bureau of Western New York, Inc., and membership manager of the Buffalo Area Chamber of Commerce [Buffalo Partnership], **BILL MARX** *also served as chair of the Western New York Peace Center and regional coordinator for Pax Christi WNY. Bill enjoys his four children, four grandchildren, and one great-grandchild.*

www.paxchristiusa.org; paxchristiwny@aol.com; (716)–462–4877

SSJ Sister Karen Klimczak Center for Nonviolence

Audrey Mang

Ten years before Sister Karen's death, the Sisters of St. Joseph and Associates of Buffalo made a *Corporate Commitment* to oppose violence and powerlessness, agreeing that in today's world this was a compelling consequence of their 350–year–old charism of "unity and reconciliation." It is the path of nonviolence that promises a way to restore relationships and harmony.

As one response to the loss of their sister, her religious community gathered a small committee to generate ideas for a suitable memorial. The work of that committee evolved into the possibility and then the reality of a Center for Nonviolence in her name. Ephesus Ministries offered space and the congregation opened the SSJ Sister Karen Klimczak Center for Nonviolence on February 3, 2007.

The Center is committed to carry on Sister Karen's vision of a world without violence, to eliminate violence in ourselves, in our society, and in our world. Sister Karen had a gift for finding ways to offer hope, to comfort the grieving, to increase awareness of violence, and to work with others to reduce violence. Continuing her efforts, the Center offers opportunities for people to learn and practice nonviolence through educational resources, youth and adult training, activities, and special events. It works in partnership with like–minded community groups that are actively promoting nonviolence. Despite the violence visited on Sister Karen, the violence raining down on our community, and the violence of wars around the globe, the Center believes that nonviolence is the future of our world. It is a future not only with less violence, but a future based on the presence of love and compassion, on unity and reconciliation, a way of life that will inspire others.

Readers and all others interested in nonviolence are invited to visit the SSJ Sister Karen Klimczak Center for Nonviolence to learn more about Sister Karen's legacy, to participate in trainings and workshops on nonviolence, and to use the Center's resources.

Available for sale at the SSJ Sister Karen Center: "Apostle of Peace: The Life of Sister Karen Klimczak, SSJ", a DVD featuring Sister Karen's vision and ministry; related Peaceprints materials (lawn signs, pins, t–shirts, note cards, ornaments) based on "NONVIOLENCE begins with ME!" *and* "I Leave PEACEPRINTS"; *copies of this book.*

SSJ Sister Karen Klimczak Center for Nonviolence*, *Vivian Ruth Waltz, Director
80 Durham Avenue, Buffalo, NY 14215. (716) 362–9688.

www.sisterkarencenter.org; info@sisterkarencenter.org

Gifts of Peaceprints

Nonviolence and Mysticism

Eastern Orthodox Icon – Julianna Ricci

"The icon is a likeness … not of corruptible flesh, but of flesh transfigured, radiant with Divine light."
(*The Meaning of Icons*, **Leonid Ouspensky**)

Nonviolence: The Essence of Our Being

Jim Mang, SSJ Associate

Sixteen months before she was murdered, I was with Sister Karen at a small dinner party. It was Christmas preparation time. Before sitting down to dinner, the host asked individuals to spend a private moment with each other in order to share some words special to that person. When I took my turn with Sister Karen, I thanked her for creating opportunities for nonviolence to happen. She responded by thanking me for promoting peace over many years. She added that we need to "let a thousand flowers bloom," or in other words we need to foster many ideas from various sources to promote nonviolence. I found out about two months later that she was already contemplating distributing "NONVIOLENCE begins with ME!" signs in the tradition of Mohandas Gandhi and Martin Luther King, Jr., who often used that phrase. One of the reasons I suggested to the Sisters of St. Joseph and Associates the establishment of a Sister Karen Klimczak Center for Nonviolence was that I saw it as a way to let a thousand nonviolent seeds bloom.

I will begin with what I observed as Sister Karen's motivation for pursuing nonviolence and then share some of my own journey in the study and practice of nonviolence. Most people thinking of and writing the word nonviolence usually form it this way: non–violence. From what I recall, Sister Karen always used nonviolence as a nonhyphenated word and idea. This is not just a semantic preference issue. Why? Because nonviolence is much, very much more than not killing or assaulting, much more than not damaging, degrading, or destroying human beings and the rest of creation.

Nonviolence is truth force, says Gandhi. It is soul force, says Martin Luther King, Jr. It is dynamic compassion, says Michael Nagler. I agree with Sister Karen: Nonviolence is the essence of our being. Violence always leads to further violence. Nonviolence always leads to peace and reconciliation. Many people see peace as the absence of war, but peace is really the presence of nonviolence. "Nonviolence is the greatest power humankind has been endowed with" (Mohandas Gandhi).

Believers and practitioners of nonviolence have come from every religion and no religion, from every age and every nation. Sister Karen was one of those special people who was open to and capable of learning from all religions, from all ages, indeed from all people with whom she came in contact. However, her primary motivation for pursuing nonviolence was the gospel of Jesus Christ. My own initiation and motivation to embrace nonviolence was a combination of the study and practice of Dr. King, Gandhi, and the social justice teachings of the Catholic Church that are rooted in the Gospels.

When biblical scholars or preachers put together lists of the essential teachings of Jesus, they usually include some or all of the following:

Luke 6:27–28 "But I say to you, love your enemies, do good to those who hate you, bless those who curse you, pray for those who abuse you."

Matthew 18:21–22 "Then Peter came up and said to him, 'Lord, how often shall my brother sin against me, and I forgive him? As many as seven times?' Jesus said to him, 'I do not say to you seven times, but seventy times seven.'"

Mark 12:28–31 "Which commandment is the first of all? Jesus answered, 'The first is, Hear, O Israel, you shall love the Lord your God with all your heart, with all your mind, and with all your strength. The second is this, you shall love your neighbor as yourself. There is no other commandment greater than these.'"

Matthew 5:23–24 "So if you are offering your gift at the altar and there remember that your brother has something against you, leave the gift there at the altar and go, first be reconciled to your brother and then come and offer your gift."

Luke 6:37 "Judge not and you will not be judged, condemn not and you will not be condemned, forgive and you will be forgiven."

Jesus does not use the word nonviolence in any of these passages or any other passages that we would call essential. But the stuff of nonviolence is in all of the passages. What is this stuff? It's love, forgiveness, reconciliation, embracing the poor, not turning our back on others. What do these qualities of nonviolence lead to? They lead to peace, personal and communal peace. When in possession of peace, we leave peaceprints wherever we go. Sister Karen died on Good Friday 2006 so others might live to spread the seeds of nonviolence. What a powerful example of the meaning of nonviolence! What an amazing grace to be witness in our own times to the presence of nonviolence!

As I wrote in the first brochure for the SSJ Sister Karen Klimczak Center for Nonviolence: "Despite the violence visited on Sister Karen, the violence that rains down on our community, and the violence of wars around the globe, we need to believe that nonviolence is the future of our world. Too many eyes focus on violence—but Sister Karen and those who believe in her vision see many signs around the world and within our own community that point to a nonviolent future. It is not just a future with less violence but a future based on the presence of love and compassion, on unity and reconciliation, a way of life that will inspire others."

Well-known for activism, Sister Karen was also a deeply spiritual person. She lived a spirituality of nonviolence that we can emulate, a spirituality that has these qualities:

> *integrity*–truth was the word Gandhi used;
>
> *concern for the poor*–how many times did Jesus say love the poor?
>
> *community*–God calls people and nations, not just individuals;
>
> *gentle spirit*–nonviolence is not achieved by harshness.

In the end, I believe that nonviolence is a way of life rooted in active compassion, a way of looking at all of life with deep empathy. It's taking on suffering rather than causing suffering.

Peace is what we all struggle to achieve. Nonviolence is the means by which we achieve peace.

JIM MANG, *an Associate member of the Sisters of St. Joseph, is one of the founders of the SSJ Sister Karen Klimczak Center for Nonviolence. He was director of the Western New York Peace Center from 1980 to 2000.*

Audrey and Jim Mang with portrait of Sister Karen

Photo – Patrick McPartland

A Light Shines in Our City

Finding a Mystic in Sister Karen's Journals

Evelyn McLean Brady

Sister Karen Klimczak became a light in our city and that light, shining and constant, is the light of a mystic. Karen would protest mightily against being identified as a mystic. I can see her in her sweatshirt and jeans, her sneakers digging in, saying, "Get a life … ." or "Forget that and move on." With apologies to Karen, I have discovered in her own words, in her sacred journals, that she indeed stands in a long and honored mother–line of Christian women mystics, and she is included for these reasons: her total surrender of self to God and her conscious experience of God's direct and transformative presence that moved her to mission.

Flame flower from Sister Karen's icon was originally found in her journal.

Firefly

Even on the darkened streets
Under sorrow's clouds that veil the sun
A light shines in our city.
Not a vigil or a street lamp,
More like a firefly
Traveling so quickly,
Unseen until she alights
In prison cell or aching heart.
A light shines in our city.

Karen is a contemplative in action. Like St. Catherine of Siena, St. Clare, St. Elizabeth of Hungary, Sojourner Truth, Mother Teresa, and Dorothy Day, to name only a few, she knows God is in all and all are in God. It was through living and working with the poor that their experience of God deepens. *I so much want to share in and with the poor, the prisoners, those who are so looked down upon by others … touch me, lift me up – make me one with those who are so much a part of me. Lord, I need to share my life with the poor and imprisoned.* She realizes that not only does she want to serve the poor, she wants to *be* the poor.

> *who touches our lives?*
> *– those who are empty of self, those who are poor,*
> *those "without" have a place for God in their lives …*
> *– Make Me Poor –*

Sister Helen Prejean tells us God is experienced in people some "want to throw away," resonating with Gandhi who believed that, when he was with the poor, he was looking into the eyes of God. In his book on Dorothy Day, Jim Forest explains: "To live with the poor is a contemplative vocation, for it is to live in the constant presence of Jesus."

Some see Karen as a saint, some as an angel. But to me, Karen is first a human being, complex, driven, and always seeking ways in the maelstrom of society to love more completely. Karen struggled with the daily responsibilities of her ministry, and yet in her work with a population that often survives on manipulation and self–deception, she longs to bring Jesus' compassion and hope to her "guys"–and to carry love to each person she meets. It is in the fire of her surrender of self that this love grows.

Surrendering to Fire
In a slow conflagration
Of her very self,
Burned away in a fire of surrender,
The light grows,
An offering to her Beloved,
The Light of the World.
A light shines in our city.

Karen's desire to live in God's life by relinquishing any trace of her false self is the *leit motif* of her journals. She prays, *God, I need to be free ... free me from myself.* And she tells God, *My love for You must supercede [sic] any reliance on self.* In another journal: *Wipe away any part of me in which my old self appears. I want to be transformed.* She has tasted the fruits of getting out of the way: *When I let you take over and use me ... so much seems to happen!* In her reflection on the Wedding Feast of Cana, she talks about the paradox of fulfillment in the emptying of self. *Cana*–

    – pitchers were empty; then Jesus filled them
    – Empty yourself of self and I will come & dwell.
    – when do we turn to the Lord?
        – in our emptiest moments

Relinquishment of self is an active, daily decision opening us to the vulnerability of suffering—and to the flow of grace. From her earliest days, Karen desired total openness to God no matter what she would be asked to give up. *When I was a teenager I remember praying to God telling Him I was willing to go anywhere, to do anything in life & I would always say for Him to use me in anyway – I was willing to go thru anything as long as I knew He was with me–anything that would transform me, purify me, enable me to grow more deeply in love with*

Him; I was so grateful for all He had given me, so grateful for the gift of life itself. Throughout the journal and in other writings, Karen reiterates the touchstone theme of her life: "You are the potter; I am the clay." She meditates on Jeremiah 18:1–6, the same scripture she would someday select for her Mass of Renewal of Vows with the Sisters of St. Joseph in 1979.

The Potter –

Lord, you are my potter; I am the clay. I have placed myself into your hands and have allowed you to mold me. So many times I've said this; so few times I've actually done it. I hurt so ... and yet that hurt, that change is GIFT, a gift I feel so very unworthy of, Lord. I recognize how you've changed me, reshaped me, always using the experiences of the past in helping it to form the new life, the new shape. It wasn't easy to "let go" then and now again I'm so AFRAID to see what new shape you may give me. Allow me to TRUST, Lord, that fear may be replaced by a desire to embrace & become whatever you may want me to become. I am clay – melt me, mold me, I'm yours.

Accepting Fire's Ash

In the embers of surrender
Blackened cinders
of weakness and faults remain.
With tenderness, she stokes this unlit residue,
Fuel transforms into new energy,
Shadows to see herself against the Son.
Ash and glittering embers
Dissolve into each other,
Each and all of her,
A light shines in our city.

If one offers her entire self to God, that totality includes weaknesses and faults. Karen knows her roadblocks to total union: her need to control; to have resolution too quickly; to judge. *I want to be in control/I'll call the shots – 'whatever you want' – that still seems to be my downfall. My favorite sin – Super Woman. What am I afraid of? ... my independence, my control, my constant need for affirmation, my fear of expressing myself; because others will see my inadequacies.* Her writings reflect the human side of a mystic–in–the–making who struggles with her shadows.

Karen's journals are a combination of prayers to God and dialogues with God, the call and response of Beloved and lover frequently identified with the experience of mystics. Yet the journals show us her humanness: *Lord help me find my keys and my sense of humor.*

The writings become her examination of conscience. – *Am I expecting too much perfection? – Am I being a coward in not saying something? /– Am I trying to be too much in control?* Karen's words reveal her very real vulnerability. *God, I need help ... I'm confused ... and feel locked up inside, unable to move ... I feel so alone. Where is everyone? Where are you God?*

The journals also give insight into Karen's experience of God. Through them, she writes to a friend, one who listens to her and assures her. Karen says to God, *I am sorry for not writing, I really want things to develop between us and I hesitate to write. God answers, Why? It's okay for you to talk to me about all the things that are happening ... Isn't that what friends are for?* When Karen is excited, God gently responds, *Let's go one–step at time – you know how over anxious you get – slow down my friend – remember doing is not important. Being is!!* Her journals become so central to her relationship with God that at one point Karen writes, *You know sometimes I feel that journaling alone can be the way for me.* But God warns, *Karen, more than anything you need to share with others – to keep your ego from becoming inflated.*

The reality of drugs and the sorrows and the violence they bring deepens Karen's dependence on her Beloved. *My heart is heavy ... why so many turning to drugs? Why so many resorting to criminal activity? Why those I feel closest to me am I being betrayed by? Help me Lord ... help me to be okay with all the struggles. Help me Lord, to become stronger in You ... am I not relying enough on You? Help me through these trials. Help me say yes to You & help me Lord especially realize You are in charge!!*

Throughout the journals we find that Karen makes mistakes, she misjudges, she second–guesses. Yet, in spite of her weaknesses and insecurities, she knows God accepts her, just as she is. *What do I fear? I fear rejection – by whom? Why? I fear not being 'good enough' and yet Lord I know in my mind you accept me as I am.* Through acceptance of her true self, embers and ash, light and darkness, oneness with the Divine deepens.

Becoming One with Fire

Each loving deed, each giving over
More wood for the fiery energy of love,
No longer her light, but God's,
A flame inseparable from fire.
One reality,
A light shines in our city.

In a reflection on John 6:51–58, the Bread of Life, Karen tells God, *Digest me, make me a very part of your life, your flow of desire, or reaching out to every part of human condition.* God responds, *... I will allow you to live ever more fully until your living and my life become one...* During Advent she writes her morning prayer: *Emmanuel – God is with us. I got up this morning & said 'God be with me.' – His answer 'I am Emmanuel – God is with you.'*

This "oneing" (a word used in the mystical tradition) explains Karen's singleness of purpose in ministry and her unitive view of life–its sorrow and its beauty. *...reaching out to every part of human condition.* Karen lives in oneness, "oneing" with her God, and that oneness becomes the life–giving and driving force of her life.

So powerful, so intimate is the realization of her oneness with the Divine that, like mystics before her, the intimacy is expressed in metaphors of pregnancy and birth. She writes, *We give Christ's birth to another...Humanity gives birth to Christ...he depends on us...waiting for us to give birth to him...he plants the seeds, he gives us himself as gifts...And asks that we give birth.*

She speaks of her reliance on God's presence: *My feelings of 'strangeness' and 'aloneness' really make me turn to You for understanding. They enable me to realize that everything can be taken away but You truly will remain with me.* God assures her, *I will be with you, always.*

The deeper her union with her Beloved, the greater her gratitude: *Lord, so often I find myself so filled with an awareness of your presence, an awareness of you taking over in my life and tears come; tears of gratitude; tears of peace; tears of unworthiness, tears of wonder.*

Karen's conversations with God range from high poetry: *Lord, my prayers shall rise like incense before you...gentle, sweet–smelling, unhesitating, reaching/risking upward, unafraid...* to informal, sweet sharings: *...hey, Lord are you ready for me?* and *It was neat to be able to show the people who came in, a bit of kindness, a bit of YOU.* She is free and comfortable in her many conversational styles because she knows her Beloved enjoys each and every facet of her. The more she becomes one with the divine presence, the more her true self emerges, the self God created her to be.

Karen's very being is galvanized into a oneness with her ministry: spreading the Good News. Her words and her actions are seamless; they do not divide, but unite. Jesus the mystic, he who is at one with the Father, is her daily teacher. Through wisdom's single eye, she sees no distinction in color or race, religion or culture, gender or class. The prayer room of Bissonette House is a place where a person could experience Native American chants, Hindu supplications, Muslim praises to Allah, Buddhist practices, and, of course, her own loving prayers to Jesus. The flames have many colors, but the fire is one.

Karen lives in the "oneness" of the eternity of each moment. There is only one moment in which to love, and it is now. In singular moments, Karen focuses her attention like a laser, whether on the terrible grief of a mother who lost her child to homicide or at her computer to organize an event to promote nonviolence. In the present moment, each person becomes sacrament. To Karen, *Time is valuable moment.* Her single–pointed attention and her total living in the "now" can perhaps partially explain her seemingly endless energy.

Like mystics before her, the Spirit catapults Karen to respond with immediacy to others without thought to her own comfort or needs. This lack of attention to self is seen in the lives of many mystics. Meister Eckhard's words, "He does not seek rest, because no unrest hinders him," resonate with Teresa of Avila's, "Love turns work into rest."

As she immerses herself more deeply in God's life, Karen seems to mine an energy field foreign to most. She speaks of her exceptional energy in her journal: *As others comment on my energy level, I comment that when God takes over and I am 'fed' by the ministry, the energy multiplies – oh, that's a good point. I can compare it to the multiplication of loaves and fishes. When we are where God wants us to be, He provides abundantly.* In her study of mystics, Carol Lee Flinders says, "All of them, to one degree or another, really did set aside personal comfort in pursuit of larger goals. ... They came to feel the suffering of others as their own, and, in working to relieve it, they experienced a mysterious enlargement, often even a kind of exaltation, regardless of the disappointment or chronic exhaustion the work itself entailed."

Being Fire

In the oxygen of love
The fire burns uncontained,
Spreading in flame–shaped doves.
A Paschal Candle now.
(May eternal light shine upon her.)
A light shines in our city.

Her profound intimacy with God unleashes in Karen a power few comprehend. Not only does it motivate her inexorable commitment to help men coming out of prison, but also it brings her to an awareness of the causes and effects of violence that literally explodes the scope of her ministry. Thus begins Karen's relentless campaign to educate for nonviolence. Nonviolence is the goal and peaceprints are the means. There is no stopping her. "The fire burned uncontained." In a journal written years before her death, Karen reflects how through fire, faith is renewed. *Yes Lord – fire needs to destroy but I'm just so conscious of how in my life, it was through the fire of destruction that a fire of faith and trust in the Lord was able to be kindled.*

Perhaps Karen's urgency lay in her realization that she would be one with Jesus not only in his mission and message but also in his death. The most poignant passages in Karen's journals presage the night of her total surrender. The following excerpts become sacred prayers, hymns, liturgy.

For the gift of the fool –
Thank you Lord ...
... give me the love needed to be a loving fool.
When they had finished making a fool of him,
they stripped him. (Matt 27–31)

Condemned though innocent, guilty of loving

Begin again ...
Knowing what I know ...
Knowing the hate I will meet for doing it,
Knowing I will be killed for it –
How great will my love have to be?

Friday Afternoon
Reach out touch
Unconditional Love
Don't be afraid to LOVE
Cross connects heaven with earth

Friday Night
NIGHT – Suffering
Love
Death
Darkness

Saturday AM
{Place}
Loneliness
It's Okay
"Limbo"

Sunday
LOVE

In her life and in her death, Sister Karen Klimczak became the love of the One to whom she totally surrendered and that love became light and that light shines in our city.

---

*A retired teacher, **EVELYN McLEAN BRADY** is a mother, a grandmother, and the wife of Hugh Brady, whom she refers to as her "theologian in residence." Evelyn is a member of Women Poets of the Crooked Circle, the Sisters of Social Service Advisory Board, the WNY Peace Center, Wellsprings (Church Women United), and is a trustee of the Rev. A. Joseph Bissonette Foundation, where she met Sister Karen Klimczak.*

References

Forrest, Jim. 2006. *Love Is The Measure.* Maryknoll, NY: Orbis Books.

Flinders, Carol Lee. 2006. *Enduring Lives: Living Portraits of Women of Faith in Action.* New York: Jeremy P. Tarcher.

Bibliography on Nonviolence

Selected and Compiled by Audrey Mang

Chacour, Elias with David Hazard. *Blood Brothers*. Tarrytown, NY: Fleming H. Revell Company, 1984. 224 pp.

> The true story of Chacour, a Palestinian Christian who has a deep love for Jews and Palestinians alike. Speaks of the root of conflict between them and the turmoil in the Middle East. Can bitter enemies ever be reconciled?

Donnelly, Doris. *Seventy Times Seven: Forgiveness and Peacemaking*. Erie, PA: Benet Press, 1993.

> Steps in the process of forgiveness, misunderstandings about and obstacles to forgiveness, and a look at "the power to forgive which comes from a place or person outside ourselves." Includes exercises.

Forest, Jim. *Making Friends of Enemies: Reflections on the Teachings of Jesus*. New York: Crossroad Publishing Company, 1987.

> An enemy is any person or group I feel threatened by; we, too, are enemies to some people. The only solution is a love characterized by action and responsibility, to foster the well–being of another whether one likes that person or not. Using the lives of Jesus, Dorothy Day, and Thomas Merton, Forest points to the spiritual liberation of turning fear into peace.

Hanh, Thich Nhat. *Creating True Peace: Ending Violence in Yourself, Your Family, Your Community, and the World*. New York: Free Press, 2003.

> Drawing on stories, his own insights, and meditation practices to teach about Right Action (acting to stop suffering), Thich Nhat Hanh emphasizes that nonviolence is not about techniques, but comes from compassion and understanding. "To practice peace, to make peace alive in us is to actively cultivate understanding, love, and compassion, even in the face of misperception and conflict. Practicing peace ... requires courage" (p. 1).

_____. Arnold Kotler. *Peace Is Every Step: The Path of Mindfulness in Everyday Life*. New York: Bantam Books, 1991.

> Writer, poet, scholar, Zen Buddhist monk, Thich Nhat Hanh tells us that we can make a difference. His way of teaching centers around the awareness of each breath and the mindfulness of each act of daily life. His creativity lies in his ability to make use of the very situations that usually pressure and antagonize us–ringing telephones, dirty dishes, traffic jams.

Kownacki, Mary Lou. OSB. *Love Beyond Measure: A Spirituality of Nonviolence*. Erie, PA: Benet Press, 1993.

> Thoughtful reflection on Sister Mary Lou's inspiring essay, "The Doorway to Peace: A Spirituality of Nonviolence," published originally in *Pax Christi USA* (Twentieth Anniversary issue, Vol. XVII, No. 1/2, Spring/Summer 1992, pp. 28–31) and regarded by many as "the fullest and most powerful expression of her insight into gospel nonviolence." Sections of her essay focus on the depth, height, length and breadth of God's Love, telling stories and bringing in world situations. The book includes material for discussion groups and offers "a prayer ritual, briefer related readings, and questions for individual reflection or group sharing" (p. *i*).

McCarthy, Coleman. *I'd Rather Teach Peace*. New York: Orbis Books, 2002.

> A journal of McCarthy's experience as a teacher provocatively offering an alternative to organized violence.

Merton, Thomas. ed. *Gandhi on Non–Violence*. [Selected texts from Mohandas K. Gandhi's *Non–Violence in Peace and War*] New York: New Directions Publishing Corporation, 1965.

> Gandhi linked the thought of East and West in his search for universal truth; for him, nonviolence sprang from realization of spiritual unity in the individual. Merton has selected the basic statements of principle and interpretation which make up Gandhi's philosophy of nonviolence (Ahimsa) and nonviolent action (Satyagraha).

Nagler, Michael. *Is There No Other Way? The Search for a Nonviolent Future*. California: Berkeley Hills Books, 2001.

> Nagler presents a clear look at the nonviolence which is found throughout history and the application of its principles to the violence of today. "Apparently there is still some primal need within us for community ... Nonviolence is the science of appealing to that need" (p. 45). "It is something absolutely everyone can use...probably the only thing we can use" (p. 73).

Sehested, Ken and Rabia Terri Harris, ed. *Peace Primer: Christian & Islamic Scripture & Tradition*. Nyack, NY: Muslim Peace Fellowship, and Charlotte, NC: Baptist Peace Fellowship of North America, 2002. [Available from Fellowship of Reconciliation, Nyack, NY.]

> An opportunity for Muslims and Christians "to listen to each other's scripture and tradition, particularly to hear what each has to say about seeking justice, pursuing peace, and working for reconciliation" (p. 3). An important contribution to Christian/Muslim understanding that grew out of joint conflict transformation trainings by the Baptist and Muslim Peace Fellowships.

Ury, William. *Getting to Peace: Transforming Conflict at Home, at Work, and in the World*. New York: Viking Penguin, 1999.

Following his previous books, *Getting to Yes* (negotiating mutually satisfactory agreements) and *Getting Past No* (negotiating with difficult people), Ury urges us to make the world safe for differences, to "change the *culture* of conflict itself within our families, our workplaces, our communities, and our world" (p. *ix*). He elaborates on the power of the Third Side, people not directly involved in the conflict who can keep the focus of both sides on shared interests and the truth of each competing point of view. "This book is about *how* and *why* we may *now*, if we choose, learn to get along" (p. *xxi*).

Vanderhaar, Gerard A. *Active Nonviolence*. Mystic, CT: Twenty–Third Publications, 1990.
A "how–to" book written for those who already believe that nonviolence offers the way to a more peaceful world, this is "an invitation to explore nonviolence in daily life, to recognize the many ways we can hurt others, to reduce those ways of being violent, substituting positive nonviolent approaches instead" (p. 22). In her introduction, Sister Joan Chittister, OSB, calls Vanderhaar's writing "manageable and understandable and profound in its implications" (p. *vii*).

_____ *Personal Nonviolence: A Practical Spirituality for Peacemakers*. Erie, PA: Pax Christi USA, 2006.
A primer on nonviolence with short, short chapters summing up a lifetime of thinking and discovery about nonviolence. Vanderhaar speaks of spirituality as "our effort to get our total being ... as right as we can given everything we know. We need a practical spirituality that will ... inspire us to contribute constructively and persevere faithfully" (pp. 8–9).

Zehr, Howard. *The Little Book of Restorative Justice*. Intercourse, PA: Good Books, 2002.
Known worldwide for his pioneering work in transforming our understandings of justice, Zehr here proposes workable "Principles and Practices" for making restorative justice both possible and useful.

Community Resources and Volunteer Opportunities

ALTERNATIVES TO VIOLENCE PROJECT
80 Durham Avenue, Buffalo, NY 14215 (716) 362–9688
info@sisterkarencenter.org; See also: www.avpusa.org; www.
avpinternational.org
*Purpose: to provide experiential workshops to help people
deal with conflict. Basic workshops develop relevant skills, and
advanced workshops focus on the underlying causes of violence.*

BACK TO BASICS OUTREACH MINISTRY
906 Broadway Avenue, Buffalo, NY 14212 (716) 854–1086.
*Purpose: to provide human resources for problems associated
with substance abuse, homelessness, gang violence, and youth
development.*

BISSONETTE HOUSE (formerly HOPE HOUSE)
335 Grider Street, Buffalo, NY 14215 (716) 892–8224
fax (716) 895–2840; www.hopeofbuffalo.org
*Purpose: to offer a supportive, transitional setting in a home-
like environment for men recently released from prison.*

CEPHAS
102 Seymour Street, Buffalo, NY 14210 (716) 856–6131
cephas@buffalo.com; www.cephas.org
*Purpose: to break the cycle of crime by assisting prisoners,
parolees, and at–risk youth to change behaviors and attitudes
which lead to imprisonment.*

COALITION FOR ECONOMIC JUSTICE
2123 Bailey Avenue, Buffalo, NY 14211 (716) 892–5877
allison_duwe@hotmail.com; www.buffalojwj.org
*Purpose: to protect the basic working rights of men and women
through the coalition of labor, religious, community leaders, as
well as youth groups and individuals.*

INTERFAITH PEACE NETWORK OF WNY
1272 Delaware Avenue, Buffalo, NY 14209 (716) 332–3904
www.ipnwny.org or http://www.ipnwny.org
*Purpose: to help faith communities in building a culture of
peace.*

KAIROS OF GREATER NIAGARA (International
ecumenical, Christian, lay–led ministry)
P.O. Box 7062, Buffalo, NY 14240
*Purpose: to give spiritual help to incarcerated individuals
in prisons. This ecumenical movement provides retreats for
inmates twice a year with weekly follow–up support.*

M. K. GANDHI INSTITUTE FOR NONVIOLENCE
500/510 Wilson Commons, Univ. of Rochester, Rochester, NY
14627 (585) 276–3787; fax (585) 276–2425
*Purpose: to educate about nonviolence and to inspire and
support efforts that promote harmony in our communities.*

PAX CHRISTI (a Catholic organization, part of PAX CHRISTI
International)
(716) 462–4877 paxchristiwny@aol.com
www.paxchristiusa.org
*Purpose: to create a world that reflects the Peace of Christ.
We reject war and every form of violence and domination. and
advocate primacy of conscience, economic and social justice,
and respect for creation.*

**P.E.A.C.E. (Parents Encouraging Accountability and
Closure for Everyone)** (716) 400–9762.
*Purpose: to provide support and assistance to families and
friends who have lost a loved one to homicide. P.E.A.C.E. seeks
to engage the authorities as they proceed through the stages of
the investigation, arrest, and prosecution of those responsible
for the murder(s).*

PRISONERS ARE PEOPLE TOO
Karima@prisonersarepeopletoo.org
www.wings.buffalo.edu/uncrownedqueens/Q/files/amin.htm
*Purpose: to engender hope through networking, action
organizing, and community building in an effort to educate the
community about criminal justice and prison issues.*

**SSJ SISTER KAREN KLIMCZAK CENTER FOR
NONVIOLENCE**
80 Durham Avenue, Buffalo, NY 14215 (716) 362–9688
info@sisterkarencenter.org; www.sisterkarencenter.org
*Purpose: to eliminate violence in ourselves, in our society, and
in our world. We work to create a nonviolent community in our
thinking, our acting, and our relationships.*

STOP THE VIOLENCE COALITION (STVC)
PO Box 626, Buffalo, NY, 14201 (716) 882–7882
stvcoalition@yahoo.com; www.stoptheviolencecoalition.com
*Purpose: to secure safe and peaceful neighborhoods by working
with gang members, and by giving lectures to block clubs,
churches, and community organizations.*

WNY PEACE CENTER (est. 1967)
2123 Bailey Avenue, Buffalo, NY 14211 (716) 894–2013
fax (716) 894–8705; www.wnypeace.org
*Purpose: to work for peace and organize for change in domestic
and foreign policy.*

WOMEN FOR HUMAN RIGHTS AND DIGNITY, INC.
2278 Main Street, Buffalo, NY 14214 (716) 831–9821
whrd2278@aol.com
*Purpose: to empower women, children, and families to move on
to economic, emotional, and social growth.*

Discussion and Reflection Questions
PEACEPRINTS: Sister Karen's Paths to Nonviolence
Apostle of Peace (DVD)

1. Which story or stories from the book stand out for you?

   What lessons or insights have you discovered in the stories you selected?

2. In Sister Karen's early family life, concern and care for others was the norm.
   a) What qualities help us develop positive relationships and bring out the best in ourselves and in others?
   b) In what ways can compassion and nonviolence be taught at an early age?

3. Sister Karen believed that Jesus' message of forgiveness is essential for true relationships, even though Sister Karen admitted her own struggles with this Gospel challenge.
   a) What examples of forgiveness in the book affected you?
   b) Share examples of forgiveness that you have heard about and why you remember them.
   c) Can you share an experience when you were able to offer or receive forgiveness?
   d) What happens when we experience forgiveness?
   e) When is it a struggle for you to forgive?

4. Central to Sister Karen's ministry was her belief in redemption, which literally translated means "being brought back" or what Sister Karen called "giving another chance."
   a) What stories of transformation or redemption in the book impacted you and what have you learned from them?
   b) Share a story from your own life of "being brought back" or being given another chance.

5. Sister Karen felt that leaving footprints was not important, but that leaving peaceprints is.
   a) What does "leaving peaceprints" mean to you?
   b) Whose peaceprints have affected you? What were they?
   c) Where/when is it most difficult for you to leave a peaceprint?
   d) What peaceprints would you like to leave? Who would be affected?

6. We are all on a journey to nonviolence. Everyone has more to learn and do—no one has arrived.
    a) What does nonviolence mean to you?
    b) How are peaceprints related to nonviolence?
    c) Who or what has been the biggest influence for you in learning about and being nonviolent?
    d) What obstacles stand in the way of your journey?

7. We often stereotype people who appear to us as "other." TV and movies help to form our opinions as well.
    a) What has been your opinion of people who are incarcerated or on parole?
    b) Is your opinion based on your own experience, people you've known, or what you've heard or read?
    c) Has anything in the book affirmed your thinking or enabled you to think differently?

8. A mystic is one who experiences God and is consciously aware of this experience.
    a) What are some characteristics of a mystic?
    b) What examples from Sister Karen's life identify her as a mystic?
    c) Do you know anyone you consider a mystic? Why do you think so?

9. What did you find most moving in the DVD, *Apostle of Peace*?

10. What would you want to talk about with Sister Karen if you could spend time with her now?

Index

Index

Index

Index

Index

Index

Index

Index

Notes